THE Leader's DIGEST

Timeless principles for team and organization success

JIM CLEMMER

THE LEADER'S DIGEST:
Timeless principles for team and organization success

DESIGN, EDITORIAL AND PRODUCTION:	MATTHEWS COMMUNICATIONS DESIGN INC.
DEVELOPMENTAL/MANAGING EDITOR:	PETER MATTHEWS
ART DIRECTOR:	SHARON MATTHEWS
INDEXER:	BARBARA SCHON

National Library of Canada Cataloguing in Publication

Clemmer, Jim, 1956-
The leader's digest : timeless principles for team and organization success / Jim Clemmer.

Includes bibliographical references and index.

ISBN 0-9684675-1-2

1. Leadership. 2. Teams in the workplace. I. Title.

HD57.7.C53 2003 658.4'092 C2003-900606-9

Published by TCG Press, an imprint of the CLEMMER Group Inc.

Printed in Canada
234567 FN 06 05 04

Contents

Acknowledgements

"Many times I realize how much my own outer and inner life is built upon the labors of my fellowmen, both living and dead, and how earnestly I must exert myself in order to give in return as much as I have received."

Albert Einstein

I owe this book, and most of my career, to the unfailing support and strong partnership of my wife Heather. Thanks so much for all you do to keep our family and business life together. You are always there – especially when the storms toss us around.

It's inspiring to watch our kids move through their sometimes turbulent teenage years and now embark on their own leadership journey. Thanks to Chris for striving to balance high achievement while living in the moment and enjoying the trip. To Jenn for setting high goals and working so hard to achieve them. To Vanessa for maintaining high energy and independence, balanced with generosity and sensitivity to others.

The CLEMMER Group owes much of its success to our ever-growing website and digital communication strategy. Our "digital diva," Julie Gil, has been the incredibly strong rock at the foundation of it all. Thanks so much for always being there and continually going way above and beyond. And thanks to Ofir for supporting Julie. Tania Robson, Betty Kaita, and Rena Lanci continue to provide support to us and to our Clients.

Many of the concepts and approaches outlined in this book have evolved through years of work and innumerable contributions from countless people at The Achieve Group, Zenger Miller, and The CLEMMER Group. Special thanks to Owen Griffiths, Mark Henderson, Derek Mendham, Debbie Poulton, Patty Schachter, Scott Schweyer, and Andrew Vujnovich.

I continue to appreciate Dave Chilton's invaluable advice and friendship. Once again, Peter and Sharon Matthews of Matthews Communications Design Inc. have provided strong editorial and design support to this book.

And thanks to so many people for sharing your stories, giving your perspectives, adding your humor, and taking action following my leadership speaking engagements, workshops, and retreats. I also appreciate the many readers of my books, our "Improvement Points" subscribers, and website visitors who send me emails with questions, suggestions, and feedback. I appreciate your perspectives and feel so privileged to journey a short way with you.

Getting to the point

"Thousands of grapes are pressed to fill one jar with wine, and the grape skin and pulp are tossed to the birds. So it is with these grapes of wisdom from the ages. Much has been filtered and tossed to the wind. Only the pure truth lies distilled in the words to come."

OG MANDINO, *THE GREATEST SALESMAN IN THE WORLD*, THE SCROLL MARKED I

Want to read up on the subject of leadership? Well, be my guest. A recent Internet search revealed that there some 10,000 leadership books in print!

What's more, it often seems that there are as many different interpretations of "leadership" as there are people using the term. The result is a confusing multitude of leadership grids, charts, formulas, jargon, fads, and buzzwords. New ones seem to pop up every week.

One of my goals in writing *The Leader's Digest* was to distill all the information on leadership down to its essentials – to provide a series of "executive summaries" or briefings on the key elements of leading people. Building on my previous work co-founding and leading the Achieve Group and now The CLEMMER Group's many years of research and writing on leadership, as well as our experiences in training and consulting with hundreds of organizations, I have attempted to identify, illustrate, and demonstrate the application of the timeless leadership principles found in our Leadership Wheel (see page 22). To do this I have used a variety of both original and classic fables or stories, real-life situations, pithy quotations, citations from current research, personal examples, and how-to points – all punctuated with whimsical illustrations and graphics.

The Leader's Digest is designed specifically for browsing, with a magazine-style presentation that allows you to leaf through the book to find the sections or approaches that are most meaningful to you. Some people, like me, are "quotaphiles" (sounds kind of suspect, I know, but it's perfectly legal) and appreciate the pithy wisdom found in a succinct quotation or turn of phrase. Others like to read the sidebars with stories, illustrations, or research. Some people like to follow the main text and then read the other areas.

It's your book and your choice.

What's new?

"A generation goes, and a generation comes, but the earth remains forever....What has been is what will be, and what has been done is what will be done; there is nothing new under the sun. Is there a thing of which it is said, 'See, this is new?' It has already been in the ages before us."

ECCLESIASTES

Historians, anthropologists and scholars of classic literature tell us that there are really just a small number of recurring stories in the entire history of humanity. Our books and movies provide us with endless variations on the basic stories of the human condition. That's one of the reasons why my favorite recreational reading is historical fiction. So many of the same themes keep showing up in the stories of people and cultures thousands of years or miles apart.

The leadership principles outlined in my books are just as timeless. They aren't new. But that doesn't make them any less important; indeed, it is the timelessness of these principles that proves their value. We need to continually rediscover and repackage them for today's circumstances.

Finding your own path

"Buddha left a road map, Jesus left a road map, Krishna left a road map, Rand McNally left a road map. But you still have to travel the road yourself."

STEPHEN LEVINE, SPIRITUALITY AND PERSONAL-GROWTH AUTHOR

After a strenuous afternoon of climbing up the face of a steep mountainside in the hot sun, two rock climbers – Pat and Andy – finally reached a plateau. It was an idyllic setting with a clear, cool glacial stream running through the alpine meadow. They had just started drinking the refreshing water and bathing in the stream when a large mountain goat came charging into the clearing and headed straight for them.

Pat's first reaction was to scramble into a nearby small cave, leaving the goat to chase after Andy, who ran halfway around the clearing and desperately climbed up a small tree. The goat began ramming the tree so hard that it was all Andy could do to hang on as it swayed back and forth. Suddenly Pat came out of his cave and ran around the clearing, yelling and shouting. The goat dashed off after Pat, almost catching up with him before Pat had made a complete circle and slipped back inside the cave. Then the goat spotted Andy, who had started down the tree. He raced over to the tree and resumed his violent ramming of the trunk.

Just as Andy was losing his grip and about to fall, Pat came running around the clearing yelling and screaming again, luring the goat away from the tree, just before diving back into the cave. The goat then spotted Andy coming down the tree and ran over to ram it again. By this time, Andy finally had a good grip on the tree. He bellowed down at Pat in the cave, "Why don't you stay in that cave and be patient. We can wait out this goat until he's tired. This too shall pass." Pat yelled back, "You wouldn't be handing out all that fancy advice if you saw the size of the bear that's sleeping in here!"

Obviously, I don't know the size of the bears in your cave. So I'm not going to attempt to give you a lot of fancy advice about how to grow your leadership. Throughout *The Leader's Digest* I will present research, experiences, illustrations, and application suggestions. It's up to you to pick what fits your situation and what doesn't.

A key part of our continuous leadership quest is finding the approaches that fit our individual values, personality, and style. It's like trying to find a path in a field of newly fallen snow. Once we walk across the field, we've discovered our path.

After years of consulting work, I realize there is no one leadership size that fits all. There are timeless principles we can all apply, but we have to make them fit our unique circumstances.

Principles in practice

Thomas Henry Huxley, the 19th-century English biologist, once said that "All truth, in the long run, is only common sense clarified." Leadership is really just common sense. The problem for most of us is that it's not common *practice*. One of my goals in writing *The Leader's Digest* is to remind us all of common-sense principles where the practicing may be slipping.

It is one thing to *know*, it's quite another to *do*. And many a manager has confused *understanding* leadership concepts with *practicing* them. Just like maintaining our physical fitness, growing our leadership is a never-ending activity.

Please visit our large and ever growing website at www.clemmer.net. We are continually adding material to make the site a major resource center for transforming personal, team, and organization performance. Join our mailing list and we will keep in touch as new programs and services spin off from The Leader's Digest, *as we update the resources on our website, and as my next books become available.* *(See page 207 for more information on our website.)*

Growth can hurt a little

Another of my goals in *The Leader's Digest* is to be a comfort-zone stretcher. In my workshops and speaking engagements, I know I've been successful when I look at the faces around me and see some measure of discomfort or resistance.

The worst response is no response. The real enemy of growth and improvement is apathy. So please let me know how this book affects you. I would love to get your personal responses to *The Leader's Digest*. Please email me directly at Jim.Clemmer@Clemmer.net.

Values. Integrity. Spirit. Energy. These are just some of the so-called "soft" qualities that characterize effective leadership – and the highly successful organizations where such qualities are respected and nurtured.

LEADERS MAKE THE DIFFERENCE

There's no avoiding it. The eternal search for sustainable competitive advantage is leading us straight into the squishy softness of culture and character. Many business people won't like it. They won't be comfortable talking with colleagues about trust, honesty, purpose, values, and other topics out of the self-help section of the bookstore. They will have to face the fact that they will likely be eaten alive by competitors who confront these issues with relish.

GEOFFREY COLVIN, "THE CHANGING ART OF BECOMING UNBEATABLE," *FORTUNE*

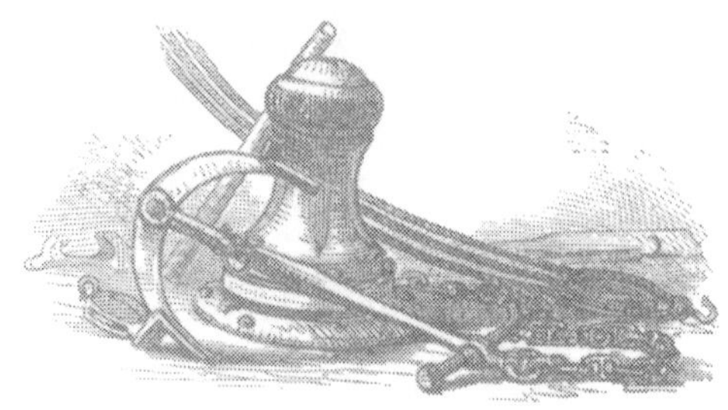

All organizations have access to more-or-less the same resources. They draw from the same pool of people in their markets or geographic areas. And they can all learn about the latest tools and techniques.

Yet not all organizations perform equally. In fact, there is a huge gap between high- and low-performing organizations. What accounts for this? Quite simply, it's people. As the venerable Peter Drucker points out, "Of all the decisions a manager makes, none are as important as the decisions about people because they determine the performance capacity of the organization."

And when it comes to people, the big difference is leadership.

Leaders are good for your health

In his book *Inspirational Leadership,* Lance Secretan reports on the role of leaders in the healthcare system:

"One hospital had significantly better results (61 predicted but 41 observed deaths) while another had significantly worse results (58% more deaths than predicted). Technically, there was very little difference between the hospitals being studied. The significant variable proved to be the quality of leadership. What the researchers found in particular was the better performing hospitals achieved superior interpersonal dynamics among the intensive care unit staff. When leaders served their [staff] well, the medical staff was able to serve their patients better. The researchers reported that 'the degree of coordination of intensive care significantly influenced its effectiveness.'"

What are people worth?

"Leadership is the art of accomplishing more than the science of management says is possible."

Colin Powell, U.S. Secretary of State

"People are our most important resource." This management cliché dates back to the beginning of the modern organization. Yet all too often it's perceived as a tired old phrase with a high "snicker factor" in many organizations. Eyes roll as the boss dutifully mouths these words.

Meanwhile, investments in assets such as physical buildings, equipment, technology, products, and strategy development vastly outstrip investments in people. Little care is given to hiring and orienting the right people. Training is often an afterthought, given little strategic consideration and even less management planning and follow-through. Performance appraisals are bureaucratic "check off the boxes" exercises that cause more angst than development. Promotions are based more on technical or management factors than on proven people-leadership abilities. Teams exist in name only. Opinions and input from frontline people are rarely sought and often discounted. Processes and systems enslave rather than enable servers or producers.

For such an "important resource," people are assigned remarkably low priority in many organizations.

The power of people

"A Wharton [School of the University of Pennsylvania] study found that 'capital investments may be a strategic necessity to stay even with the competition,' but the investments in workers yielded far greater returns. Says Patrick Harker, one of the study's authors: 'Machines can't give you a competitive advantage. It's all about people.'"

From Fortune *magazine, in "What Makes a Company Great," a survey of the world's most admired companies:*

An MIT global auto industry study found that a major reason Toyota's productivity is far ahead of Nissan is because Nissan poured money into robots and computers while Toyota focused on people and processes (mainly through Kaizen). Toyota then used automation to support its people and processes.

A major international company studied their worker compensation claims and attitude surveys and found that where supervisors and managers are perceived to be more caring about people injuries and compensation, claims were much lower.

In the most admired companies, the key priorities were teamwork, customer focus, fair treatment of employees, initiative, and innovation. In average companies the top priorities were minimizing risk, respecting the chain of command, supporting the boss, and making budget.

Can a great leader be an effective manager? Or vice versa? While each requires different abilities, they need not be – and should not be – mutually exclusive. Both are essential for peak organizational performance.

MANAGEMENT VS. LEADERSHIP

Leadership and management are two distinctive and complementary systems of action. Each has its own function and characteristic activities. Both are necessary for success in an increasingly complex and volatile business environment… strong leadership with weak management is no better, and is sometimes actually worse, than the reverse. The real challenge is to combine strong leadership and strong management and use each to balance the other.

JOHN KOTTER, MANAGEMENT/LEADERSHIP AUTHOR AND PROFESSOR OF ORGANIZATIONAL BEHAVIOR, HARVARD BUSINESS SCHOOL

The terms "management" and "leadership" are often interchanged. In fact, many people view them as basically the same thing. Yet management is as distinct from leadership as day is from night. Both are necessary, however, for a high-performance organization. By contrasting them and understanding their differences, we can better balance and improve these essential roles.

One key distinction between management and leadership is that we manage *things* and lead *people*. Things include physical assets, processes, and systems. People include customers, external partners, and people throughout our team or organization (or "internal partners"). When dealing with things, we talk about a way of *doing*. In the people realm, we're talking about a way of *being*.

COMPLEMENTARY STRENGTHS

Management	**Leadership**
Processes	People
Facts	Feelings
Intellectual	Emotional
Head	Heart
Position power	Persuasion power
Control	Commitment
Problem solving	Possibility thinking
Reactive	Proactive
Doing things right	Doing the right things
Rules	Values
Goals	Vision
Light a fire under people	Stoke the fire within people
Written communications	Verbal communications
Standardization	Innovation

Both management and leadership are needed to make teams and organizations successful. Trying to decide which is more important is like trying to decide whether the right or left wing is more important to an airplane's flight. I'll take both please!

Getting technical

In The CLEMMER Group's consulting and training work we often add a third element – technical – to management and leadership to form what we call a "Performance Triangle." This adds another dimension to the question, "how should the organization's focus be allocated to each area?" While apparently simple, the question is often a very difficult one to answer, since there is no universal formula that applies to all organizations. Some need more technical skills or better technologies. Others need the discipline of better systems and processes. Most need a lot more leadership.

Another complicating factor is that needs are easily misidentified. For example, we have found that most organizations have communication problems of one kind or another. Often these are seen as leadership issues. Many times they are. But just as often the roots of the problem are intertwined with poor processes, systems, or structure – all of which are management issues.

The triangle depicts the balance between the three critical success factors. Imagine a pendulum swinging in the center of the triangle. It's very difficult to keep the pendulum in a state of equilibrium. In some cases, organizations may need to swing the pendulum in one direction because that's where it's weakest. For example, entrepreneurial start-up companies often have strong

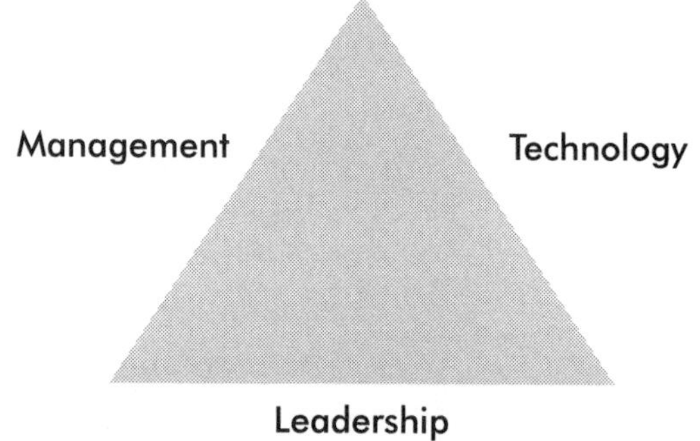

vision, passion, and energy (leadership) and may also have good technological or technical skills. But their lack of systems and processes or poor management discipline leads to a lot of errors, poor service/quality, and frustration for customers and people in the organization.

The most common weakness, however, is in leadership. The triangle illustrates that a well-balanced organization has leadership at the base. This allows management and technology to serve rather than enslave producers, servers, and customers.

Push or pull?

Warren Bennis, Professor of Business Administration at the University of Southern California, has been extensively studying and writing about leadership for many decades. He explains why leaders are so much more successful than managers in harnessing people power: "Management is getting people to do what needs to be done. Leadership is getting people to want to do what needs to be done. Managers push. Leaders pull. Managers command. Leaders communicate."

Leadership is first and foremost a way of being. It begins at the center and extends outward, following the timeless leadership principles.

The Leadership Wheel

The winds and waves are always on the side of the best navigators.

Edward Gibbon, English historian

Leaders look beyond the current situation – beyond what is to what could be. That's why leadership is all about change. It's why leadership is action, not a position.

Growing our leadership is also a dynamic process. It begins at the center of our being and develops in multiple directions, each represented by the timeless leadership principles described in this book. This "hub and spokes" model is the basis for The CLEMMER Group's Leadership Wheel.

Each part of the wheel corresponds to an area of leadership. At the hub of the wheel, we have the vision, values, and purpose with which leaders effectively focus their teams and organizations on the core of their being (Chapter 2: Focus and Context).

Leaders also take initiative and do what needs to be done rather then waiting for "them" to do something (Chapter 3: Responsibility for Choices).

Leaders are authentic and lead by visible example, fostering openness and continuous feedback (Chapter 4: Authenticity).

Leaders are passionate and build strong commitment through involvement and ownership (Chapter 5: Passion and Commitment).

Leaders lead with heart and rouse team or organizational spirit (Chapter 6: Spirit and Meaning).

Leaders grow people through strong coaching and continuous development (Chapter 7: Growing and Developing).

Finally, leaders energize people by building strong teams, inspiring, and serving (Chapter 8: Mobilizing and Energizing).

The wheel model provides a metaphor for situations faced by an organization. For example, just as a wheel's weight-bearing ability depends upon the strength of its hub, so too does the strength of an organization's hub (or core values) determine the weight of the performance and change issues that it is able to carry.

The wheel also represents the circular nature of leadership – there is no beginning or end. Each of the supporting leadership principles around the outside of the Leadership Wheel are interdependent and interconnected. If our team or organization develops all the leadership skills, the wheel is well-rounded. If it is deficient in one or more of these skills, the ride may be a little bumpy.

The timeless leadership principles make intuitive sense. When we look at the key factors for most organizational success, we generally find these principles at work.

SOFT SKILLS, HARD RESULTS

We should take care not to make the intellect our god. It has, of course, powerful muscles, but no personality. It cannot lead, it can only serve.

ALBERT EINSTEIN

Leadership deals with the world of emotions and feelings. It is more of an art than a science. Like artists, leaders have the ability to share their vision of the world. Leaders influence our perceptions and help us look at situations in new ways. These skills – and the leadership principles that guide their development – are critical to the success of an organization or team.

Leading by emotion

Daniel Goleman, Richard Boyatzis, and Annie McKee have conducted extensive research into the rapidly growing number of studies on the pivotal role of emotional intelligence. They have found that in 50 to 70 percent of all cases, leaders are directly responsible for how people in an organization or team perceive their culture. As they state in their book, *Primal Leadership: Realizing the Power of Emotional Intelligence,* "Leaders have always played a primordial emotional role. No doubt humankind's original leaders – whether tribal chieftains or shamanesses – earned their place in large part because their leadership was emotionally compelling. . .the leader acts as the group's emotional guide. . . in any human group the leader has maximal power to sway everyone's emotions. If people's emotions are pushed toward the range of enthusiasm, performance can soar; if people are driven toward rancor and anxiety, they will be thrown off stride."

Emotional intelligence has profound implications for leaders and their organizations. "This emotional task of the leader is primal – that is, first – in two senses: It is both the original and the most important act of leadership."

Of course, there are some people who remain unconvinced of the value of these "soft skills." They're typically managers with minimal leadership qualities, who prefer to focus on being bottom-line driven, strategists, marketing aces, technical experts, "snoopervisors," and so on.

These managers often talk about the importance of personal effectiveness and development. They pledge undying allegiance to values, mission, and vision. They go on about people issues, like communication, teamwork, respect, and service. But they really think it's just a lot of fluff.

Well, maybe they should think again.

Now there is hard evidence that those "soft" leadership principles are *the* major factor in what makes a high-performance team or organization. The exciting and rapidly expanding research on emotional intelligence shows that a leader's personal characteristics and leadership competencies have a direct bearing on his or her personal performance – as well as on that of their team and organization. For example, studies show that even a leader's mood is highly contagious. Depending on whether he or she is upbeat and supportive, or cranky and disapproving, the team will either be charged with high achievement or poisoned with deadly toxins.

Improving our emotional intelligence

"There now is a considerable body of research suggesting that a person's ability to perceive, identify, and manage emotion provides the basis for the kinds of social and emotional competencies that are important for success in almost any job. Furthermore, as the pace of change increases and the world of work makes ever greater demands on a person's cognitive, emotional, and physical resources, this particular set of abilities will become increasingly important."

CARY CHERNISS, RUTGERS UNIVERSITY

There's not a lot we can do about the processing power between our ears. For the most part, we're stuck with whatever intelligence quotient (IQ) we've got. The good news for many of us is that our IQ is dramatically less important to success and happiness than our emotional intelligence (EQ). What's even better is that EQ, unlike IQ, can be improved. It's not easy (nothing worth doing ever is), but it can be done.

As University of Toronto psychology professors Steven Stein and Howard Book (what better name for an author?) write in their book, *The EQ Edge: Emotional Intelligence and Your Future*, "We know that emotional intelligence can be enhanced because we've seen it happen over and over again as we've worked with corporate CEOs and other executives, school teachers, military personnel, counselors and consultants, mental health professionals and husbands and wives. Adopting proven methods found in cognitive and behavioral therapy, as well as from psychodynamic theory, we have trained many of these individuals to increase their emotional intelligence in easily understandable and proven ways."

Improving our emotional intelligence starts with a clear picture of our ideal self. This is at the hub of our Leadership Wheel: Where am I going (or what is the picture of my *preferred* future)? The next step is a "gap analysis," or assessment of my current strengths and weaknesses, followed by a plan for bridging those gaps (building on my strengths and strengthening my weaknesses). Then the real improvement work begins – experimenting with new behaviors, reframing my thinking, developing skills, and mastering feelings. This can often be reinforced by forming new relationships or by changing the dynamic of existing ones. These steps are generally difficult to sustain on our own. That's why personal coaches, counselors, and consultants have become so popular. They help us step back from the movie of our life to review and reset our thinking and actions.

Studies in EQ

From "The Business Case for Emotional Intelligence," by Cary Cherniss, Rutgers University, from the website of the Consortium for Research on Emotional Intelligence (www.eiconsortium.org):

Competency research in over 200 companies and organizations worldwide shows that about one-third of the vast difference between high and low performers (top performers are 12 times more productive than those at the bottom and 85 percent more productive than the average performer) is due to technical skill and cognitive ability while two-thirds is due to emotional competence. In top leadership positions, over four-fifths of the difference is due to emotional competence.

A study of 515 senior executives found emotional intelligence was a better predictor of success than either relevant previous experience or high IQ. More specifically, the executive was high in emotional intelligence in 74 percent of the successes and only in 24 percent of the failures. The study included executives in Latin America, Germany, and Japan, and the results were almost identical in all three cultures.

An analysis of more than 300 top-level executives from fifteen global companies showed that six emotional competencies distinguished stars from the average: Influence, Team Leadership, Organizational Awareness, Self-Confidence, Achievement Drive, and Leadership.

From Steven Stein and Howard Book, *The EQ Edge: Emotional Intelligence and Your Success:*

Over the past five years, MHS, in cooperation with Reuven and other researchers worldwide, has administered the EQ-I to almost 42,000 people in 36 countries, building up a voluminous data bank and uncovering incontrovertible links between emotional intelligence and proven success in people's personal and working lives.

A survey of over 700 multi-millionaires asked each one to rate 30 factors most responsible for their success. The top five were all attributes of emotional intelligence. IQ was 21st on the list.

POINTS OF ORIGIN

Where do we want to go? What are the beliefs that will guide us in getting there? Why do we want to get there at all? These are the central questions of leadership. They provide an organization's

FOCUS AND CONTEXT

Successful leaders spend a lot of time creating the identity of the organization – what our values are, what our mission is, what our purpose is, how we are going to act together as one. Those are agreements of how we are going to be together. You can actually get a whole team or a whole group to hold one another accountable. The team self-regulates and members call each other in a much more immediate way than a leader can ever do.

MARGARET WHEATLEY, PRESIDENT OF THE BERKANA INSTITUTE, A GLOBAL CHARITABLE LEADERSHIP FOUNDATION

It wasn't by accident that we chose to arrange the timeless leadership principles in the shape of a wheel. Of all the principles, there is one that is central, one from which the others emanate, much as spokes radiate from the hub of a wheel. That core principle is Focus and Context.

Microsoft chairman Bill Gates kept a clear and consistent focus for his company as it pioneered a new industry. He found that "maintaining focus is a key to success. You should understand your circle of competence and spend your time and energy there... I've learned that only through focus can you do world-class things, no matter how capable you are."

So what is this all-important principle? In fact, it consists of three interrelated parts, which are defined by the answers to three key questions:

1 Where are we going (the **vision** or picture of our preferred future or outcome)?

2 What do we believe in (our guiding **values** or principles)?

3 Why do we exist (our reason for being, mission, or **purpose**)?

These questions are about as simple as I can make them. And this is important, because they can become overly complicated. Over the years I've engaged in too many "vernacular engineering" debates with colleagues and management teams that get enmeshed in numerous definitions of visions, values, mission statements, and the like. Too often we are just splitting hairs (which, given my follicular challenges, is something I really can't afford to do) without really adding value to our understanding and application of the important leadership principles. So I usually try to reduce Focus and Context to its key components, using these terms: Vision, Values, and Purpose.

Frederick Smith, Chairman and CEO of FedEx, created a whole new industry when he began his company in 1973. Smith's idea of locating a central hub in Memphis, Tennessee, to provide overnight courier service across the U.S. was a radical departure from traditional thinking – so radical, in fact, that when he outlined the concept in a paper at business school, his professor gave him a C. (The idea was too unworkable, he said.) Smith's long and highly successful career as both a start-up entrepreneur and operating CEO (a very rare combination) has led him to conclude, "The primary task of leadership is to communicate the vision and the values of an organization. Second, leaders must win support for the vision and the values they articulate. And third, leaders have to reinforce the vision and the values. That's probably the most difficult task, and it's where most organizations fall apart."

Focus and Context is where the contrast between management and leadership is possibly at its sharpest. It is the very beginning point of strong leadership. Consider, for example, all the people you know well, and identify those you think of as being strong leaders. What characteristics do they share? Chances are they don't just wait for things to happen to them; they go and make things happen. They don't just follow the crowd; they blaze their own trail. They don't wait to be told what to do; they do what needs to be done. Leaders seldom waffle or vacillate. They are purposeful and deliberate.

Within the workplace, a leader typically has a clear mental picture of what success looks like for a particular project or, more generally, for a successful team or the organization as a whole. He or she is able to "emotionalize" that picture and bring it alive for people. Leaders impart a sense of trust and credibility by living true to a core set of values or guiding principles – even if they haven't articulated and labeled them. People respond to this leadership because they can clearly see the principles from which it flows.

Leaders always inspire a response, whether positive or negative. They move forward with purposeful action that, like a powerful magnet, both attracts and repels. Those people who are excited by the vision join the team and add to a powerful coalition. Those who are lukewarm or turned off by the vision, values, and purpose quickly turn away. Few are left indifferent and apathetic.

Leading change from the core

"Leadership is about coping with change. Part of the reason it has become so important in recent years is that the world has become more competitive and more volatile... doing what was done yesterday, or doing it 5% better, is no longer a formula for success. Major changes are more and more necessary to survive and compete effectively in this new environment. More change always demands more leadership."

JOHN KOTTER, "WHAT LEADERS REALLY DO," *HARVARD BUSINESS REVIEW*

Change is a fact of life. And as the pace of change accelerates, organizations are being pulled in many directions by factors such as new technologies, customer demands, e-commerce, workforce demographics, business model challenges, fierce competition, shareholder expectations, shrinking cycle times, and shifting work ethics. Now, more than ever, organizations need the bonding glue of a strong culture to hold everything and everyone together.

At the core of that culture is a strong leader who knows where he or she wants to lead their organization, but is highly flexible and opportunistic in pulling teams together to try new approaches, to experiment, and to learn (as well as occasionally fail) their way to success. The hub of their leadership wheel is solidly built around a compelling vision, core values, and an energizing purpose.

Uncertainty principles

"We are forever looking for a cure for our ills. We do this by placing ourselves in the position of manager, of thus managing change. Unless it is managed, something is wrong. But our real unconscious and underlying wish is to find a cure for the impermanence of life, and for that there is no remedy."

David Whyte, *The Heart Aroused: Poetry and Preservation of the Soul in Corporate America*

"True genius resides in the capacity for evaluation of uncertain, hazardous, and conflicting information."

Winston Churchill

"Maturity of mind is the capacity to endure uncertainty."

John Finlay

"The quest for certainty blocks the search for meaning. Uncertainty is the very condition to impel man to unfold his powers."

Erich Fromm

Leading change can be a lot like sailing a ship. We start off by setting our destination, establishing a course, and heading in that direction. In calm seas, we can sit back and sail smoothly along. But in rough seas, we often find ourselves off-course, harnessing the shifting winds, dealing with varying currents, or navigating hazards. We may have to batten down the hatches and keep the bow pointed into the waves as we battle an unexpected storm. Other times there is no wind and we just bob adrift in the waters. At all times we need to be watching for new dangers, checking our location, following basic nautical principles, and constantly steering so we're not swamped by the ever-changing waves.

Sight lines

"Men who look on nature, and their fellow-men, and cry that all is dark and gloomy, are in the right; but the somber colors are reflections from their own jaundiced eyes and hearts."

CHARLES DICKENS, *OLIVER TWIST*

TEAM MEMBERS LEARN WHAT THEY LIVE

If a team member lives with fear,
He learns to avoid risk-taking.

If a team member lives with power,
She learns to resist change.

If a team member lives with mistrust,
He learns to be suspicious

If a team member lives with control,
She learns how to beat the rules.

If a team member lives with small expectations,
He learns to have a limited horizon.

If a team member lives strictly within reality,
She learns to focus only on what is.

If a team member lives with leadership,
He learns how to take initiative.

If a team member lives with inspiring visions,
She learns how to climb out of reality ruts.

If a team member lives with core values,
He learns how to set priorities.

If a team member lives with a meaningful purpose,
She learns how to tap into a deeper energy.

If a team member lives with growth and learning,
He learns how to manage change.

If a team member lives with participation,
She learns how to be a valued partner.

If a team member lives with emotional intelligence,
He learns how to be a leader.

JIM CLEMMER, INSPIRED BY DOROTHY LAW NOLTE'S POEM, "CHILDREN LEARN WHAT THEY LIVE"

Management deals with the here and now. Leadership looks beyond the present, to imagine what could be.

VISION

At first people refuse to believe that a strange new thing can be done, then they begin to hope it can be done, then they see it can be done – then it is done and all the world wonders why it was not done centuries before.

FRANCES HODGSON BURNETT, 19TH-CENTURY AMERICAN WRITER

Thomas Kuhn, the noted American professor of the philosophy and history of science, is best known for his work, *The Structure of Scientific Revolutions*, which sold over 1 million copies in 16 languages. The book challenged conventional thinking that scientific change was strictly a rational process. It also popularized use of the term "paradigm" as the mental model or framework scientists use to explain laws of nature. Paradigms are essential for learning and continuously improving upon theories and their applications.

However, paradigms are also very limiting. According to Kuhn, "What a person sees depends upon what he looks at and what his previous experience has taught him." Many scientists – especially those with the most time and training invested in an established scientific discipline – resist new paradigms that challenge their established view of how the world works. They often ignore or just don't see new contradictory evidence that doesn't fit their paradigm.

When he was three years old, our son Chris had an unusual way of dealing with parental authority. Upon being told to stop doing something he shouldn't do, he would quickly cover his eyes. If he couldn't see you, then he could carry on as if you weren't there.

Many organizations like to talk about "thinking outside the box." Yet the role of managers is typically to improve on the accepted paradigm, or what is "inside the box." They focus on what is, and work hard to enhance it. That's extremely important and vital to orderly processes and systems that consistently deliver high-quality products or services. Leaders, on the other hand, are more inclined to smash old boxes or paradigms and construct new ones. Kuhn found that scientific paradigms don't build on previous ones, they sweep them away. That's often the case with new organizational paradigms as well. Strong leaders focus less on improving what *is* (established products or services, for example) than on seeing what *could be*.

Managers set goals, leaders have vision

"Nothing happens unless first we dream."

CARL SANDBURG, AMERICAN WRITER

Just as the terms "management" and "leadership" are often used interchangeably, goals and visions are often perceived to be the same thing. They are not. While both are critical to success (and are therefore highly interconnected), the management act of goal-setting is quite different from the leadership act of visioning.

GOALS	VISION
Appeal to our intellect	Engages our emotions
Results and timeframes	A desired future state
Builds a business case	Kindles a cause
Rational	Intuitive
Pushes performance	Inspires and aligns
Targets and objectives	Images and feelings
Solves problems	Imagines possibilities
Logical progression	Irrational "skyhooks"
Written	Verbal

Goals and vision are different, but co-dependent. Visioning without goal-setting and action is day-dreaming. Goal-setting without the broader context of an exciting vision is drudgery.

O. A. Ohmann, an executive at Standard Oil, coined the term "sky-hook" to describe the vision and courage required to develop a new paradigm. "It came in the heat of a discussion with a group of business executives attending the Institute of Humanistic Studies at Aspen, Colorado. As we debated the limits of the rational and scientific approach to life, it occurred to me that science appears rational on the surface, but at its very foundation typically lies a purely intuitive nonrational assumption made by some scientist. He just hooked himself on a piece of the sky out there and hung on. It was a complete leap of faith that led him."

The limits of planning

"Imagination is the beginning of creation. You imagine what you desire, you will what you imagine and at last you create what you will."
George Bernard Shaw

No one disputes the importance of planning. It is a key management skill. It is critical to team or organizational success. But in most organizations, traditional forecasting and planning methods are limited by the fact that they treat the future as an extension of the present. As such, they serve to reinforce existing paradigms. This blocks change and keeps people focused on the continuous expansion of what is. As a result, the organization is less inclined to consider new possibilities that might point in different direction – away from *what is* and toward *what could be*.

Traditional planning tries to take the uncertainty out of life by forecasting the future. Yet this is clearly impossible. As the old Yiddish proverb teaches us, "*Mensch tracht; Gott lacht*" (Man plans; God laughs).

In *The Fortune Sellers: The Big Business of Buying and Selling Predictions,* William Sherden reports on his extensive study of the multi-decade track record of forecasting: "Of these sixteen types of forecasts, only two – one-day-ahead weather forecasts and the aging of the population – can be counted on; the rest are about as reliable as the fifty-fifty odds in flipping a coin. And only one of the sixteen – short-term weather forecasts – has any scientific foundation." He concludes, "Even with all the advances in science and technology that are available to them, the experts are not getting any better at prediction. In some respects, we are hardly better off than the Romans or Greeks, who read animal entrails to make major decisions regarding the future."

Walt Disney provides a well-known illustration of vision in action. He declared, "If you can dream it, you can do it. Always remember that this whole thing was started by a mouse."

When he was a creative director at Walt Disney Studios, Mike Vance liked to tell the story of a conversation he had shortly after the opening of Disney World, the Florida theme park that had once been nothing more than bush and swampland. He remembers someone saying to him, "Isn't it too bad Walt Disney didn't live to see this." Vance replied, "He did see it – that's why it's here."

Successful entrepreneurs are good examples of strong leaders who use vision to build new paradigms. Entrepreneurs know that there can only be experts on what was or is. There are no experts on what will be. One highly successful entrepreneur declared, "I am not a disciple of research – unless, of course, it agrees with me. Otherwise it's useless." Successful entrepreneurs are leaders with vision who predict the future by inventing it.

English artist and poet William Blake once observed, "What is now proved was once only imagined." Entrepreneurs sell their imaginings to investors, customers, team members, creditors, partners, or anyone who can help make their dreams a reality. They may put business plans together to satisfy investors or bankers, but mostly they are "hooking themselves to a piece of the sky and hanging on." They energize and rally people around the dream and make it into a self-fulfilling prophecy.

Vision at work

"Vision is one of the least understood – and most overused – terms in the language... when you have superb alignment, a visitor could drop into your organization from another planet and infer the vision without having to read it on paper."

JIM COLLINS, AUTHOR OF *BUILT TO LAST* AND *GOOD TO GREAT*

Imagine the possibilities...

Strong leaders make people hopeful about the future. As editor and writer Norman Cousins reflects, "The capacity for hope is the most significant fact of life. It provides human beings with a sense of destination and the energy to get started." Hope is a key activator. When faced with major changes, leaders optimistically focus everyone's attention on the possibilities. They look for signs of progress and reinforce those to build forward momentum. A compelling vision of the team or organization's preferred future keeps people from obsessing over present-day obstacles or getting stuck in the past.

Picture this...

Research in psychology and medicine has given us insights into such phenomena as the placebo effect, as well as created the tongue-twisting specialty of psychoneuroimmunology – all of which has proven a very strong cause-and-effect relationship between our minds (vision or expectations) and our health, happiness, and performance.

Strong leaders inspire performance by reaching people's imaginations with vivid images. They use physical models, stories, metaphors, examples of past successes, descriptive language – alone or in combination, with plenty of repetition – to help people form a compelling mental picture of where the team or organization is headed.

Envisioning high performance

At The CLEMMER Group, we have been working with Peter Jensen, one of the nation's top sports psychologists, and his organization, to deliver their powerful program, called "Coaching for High Performance," to our clients. After decades of experience advising professional and amateur coaches – as well as many Olympic athletes – Peter has found that the best coaches are those who can help their athletes or teams clearly see the performance levels they are shooting for. "Imagery is the language of performance," Peter declares. "Until people can see what needs to be done and themselves performing the steps to doing it, they can't perform."

Do you see what I see?

Rapid shifts in the marketplace had made it necessary for the company to overhaul its line of products and services. The company's management team had been working very hard to make the necessary changes, but the members of the team seemed to be laboring at cross-purposes and constantly tripping over each other. We were called in to assess the underlying causes and to help them take a new approach. Our investigation soon revealed that the teamwork problem derived from incompatible views of the company's new business model, as well as its product and service strategies. It was as if all the managers were attempting to put together a giant jigsaw puzzle, with each assigned to pieces of a specific color – some green, some brown, others blue, and so on – with the result that each team had a different idea of what the finished puzzle should look like. Those working on the green pieces thought the puzzle was a mountain scene. The blue-piece group thought they were working on a seascape. The people working on the brown pieces thought the puzzle was a country garden.
The solution was to restore their collective vision so that everyone was looking at the same picture.

All together now...

Great teams and organizations rally around a shared vision. Team members feel connected and proud to be involved. Strong leaders know and care about the people on their teams. They have frequent discussions about each person's individual goals and performance objectives. These coaching conversations help the leader see the extent to which each person understands and buys into the vision. It's also an opportunity to clarify the vision and further increase the "buy-in" factor. These leaders then look for every opportunity to align that individual's strengths and aspirations with the vision of the organization or team. The vision helps to define a performance standard that inspires creative approaches and stretches performance targets. Adds Cynthia Tragge-Lakra, manager of executive development at General Electric, "Leaders need to energize people so that they rally behind the vision and take leadership roles themselves in bringing that vision to life."

Failing forward

After a series of experiments failed to produce the outcome he expected, Thomas Edison was asked what results he had to show for all the time and money invested. "Results?" he replied indignantly, "Why, man, I've gotten a lot of results. I know several thousand things that won't work. I am not discouraged, because every wrong attempt discarded is another step forward. Just because something doesn't do what you planned to do doesn't mean it's useless."

Don't just sit there planning, try something...

Successful leaders broadly share their vision and encourage team members to experiment, pilot, and muck around looking for the pathways that will lead them to make that vision a reality. If the vision represents a significant stretch or paradigm shift, there's no management planning processes that will be able to lay down a sure course of action to success. Years of research on the nature of innovation shows that what look like brilliant moves in retrospect were often accidents. If we're not failing regularly, we're not doing anything innovative. If we only walk in the tracks of others we'll never make any new discoveries. True failure is not capitalizing on our mistakes, setbacks, and things that didn't turn out as we planned.

Oh, the Place You'll Go

Congratulations!
Today is your day.
You're off to Great Places!
You're off and away!

You have brains in your head.
You have feet in your shoes.
You can steer yourself
any direction you choose.

Dr. Seuss, *Seuss-isms for Success*

An organization's culture is defined by its core ideals and beliefs – not just declared, but acted upon.

VALUES

No men can act with effect who do not act in concert; no men can act in concert who do not act with confidence; no men can act with confidence who are not bound together with common opinions, common affections, and common interests.

EDMUND BURKE, 18TH-CENTURY BRITISH STATESMAN

During the 1980s, when I was co-founder and leader of The Achieve Group, we worked with California-based Zenger Miller and Tom Peters to implement a culture-change process based on Peters' and Bob Waterman's book, *In Search of Excellence*. Adding to, and building upon, the work of their McKinsey & Company colleagues, Terrence Deal and Allan Kennedy, Peters and Waterman showed that the cultures of excellent companies are grounded in core values.

The idea of clarifying core values was new for many management teams at the time. We helped hundreds of teams in centering their change- and improvement-effects around their vision, as well as a set of three to five core values that best defined the culture they were trying to reinforce, change, or improve.

Today it's a rare organization that doesn't have a set (most often a laundry list) of values. In fact, values have become one more item added to the requisite organization checklist (Organization chart? Check. Strategic plan? Check. Budget? Check. Vision statement? Check. Values? Check). Frequently when we ask about the organization's values, a dusty old piece of paper is produced. Quite often this is followed by a debate about whether or not this is the right version of the organization's values.

Bringing values to life

> *"Values are the bedrock of any corporate culture. As the essence of a company's philosophy for achieving success, values provide a sense of common direction for all employees and guidelines for day-to-day behavior… often companies succeed because their employees can identify, embrace, and act on the values of the organization."*
>
> TERRENCE DEAL AND ALLAN KENNEDY, *CORPORATE CULTURES: THE RITES AND RITUALS OF CORPORATE LIFE*

Many organizations can point to a list of values. The real question is how the values are lived. Have we just done our "values thing" during a planning session or are they actively used in our daily operations? Do they have a high "snicker factor" to be greeted with rolled eyes when they are occasionally brought forward? As a manager have I "Dilbertized" my workplace by going through the motions of periodically referring to vision, values, and purpose when the leadership spotlight is turned on us or when it is annual planning time again?

A key test of whether core values are alive and real in an organization is to ask team members at random to recite those values. If they can't do it without referring to a piece of paper, there are either too many values (ideally they should be no more than three or four words or short phrases – five if you really stretch it) or they aren't being used in daily operations.

Here are some examples of how highly effective leaders keep core values alive.

- Make "values fit" a key criterion in hiring. Most effective leaders know that you can improve a person's skills and experience with training and development, but it's much harder to train for attitude and almost impossible to change a person's core values.

- Replace rules and policies with values and trust. Effective leaders treat team members as responsible adults who want to do the right thing for the team or organization. They know that with good support, training, and examples to follow, most people will exercise good judgment. The exceptions can be dealt with on an as-needed basis. This principle can also extend to customers. For example, we know of one courier company that automatically sends customers up to $300 for any damage claims. Experience has shown that customers are dishonest less than 1% of the time.

- Promote only those people who are role models for the organization's values. Promotions are the clearest indication of whether values are lived or simply espoused. All too often, a manager will declare the values of teamwork, customer service, and trust, but then promote someone who is the meanest SOB in the place, manages by email, rarely sees customers or team members, and "snoopervises" rules like the Gestapo – simply because he or she gets the job done. In such cases, it becomes evident just how important (or unimportant) lived values really are.

Early in my career I found work that was a great fit for my skills and interests. I grew and moved through the company to ever-higher levels of responsibility. I was especially lucky to be mentored by a senior manager who coached and developed my skills, and brought out more potential in me than I realized I had at the time. Her trust and faith in me built my confidence and a strong foundation for future growth.

After one promotion that would take me across the country to manage the company's largest branch, I spent a week introducing John, the new president (he was also new to me, since he came from another part of the company), to the various field managers I served and supported with my internal training and consulting work.

It quickly became embarrassing to be with him. He was an obnoxious boor who had all the answers – often to questions he wasn't even asked. His personal time management was a joke. One morning, at the time we were to leave for a meeting, I had to rouse him from bed by pounding on his hotel room door (he'd been "out on the town" the night before). His honesty and ethics were questionable – you really did want to count your fingers after shaking his hand (or at least wash your hands very thoroughly). He was an elitist who treated frontline team members as "the little people."

I subsequently moved 2,000 miles away from him and head office to assume new responsibilities at one of our branch offices. Since he was clearly an out-of-sight-out-of-mind manager I was thankful for the distance that separated us. But since I did report to him, I was still obliged to maintain contact through periodic phone conversations and occasional meetings.

During one of those meetings, some 12 months after moving from head office, we talked about the state of the company and his activities over the past year. I'd been hearing stories of his awful management behavior and the deteriorating condition of the whole Canadian operation. His stories of "conquests," conflicts, "housecleaning," and frustrations with the "unbelievable number of idiots out there" confirmed my worst fears. This guy was a disaster. My initial assessment of him had been, if anything, too charitable.

John did me a big favor that afternoon in his office. His complete lack of leadership and subsequent performance problems confirmed my growing belief in "people power." Since I couldn't in good conscience belong to a management team that had a leader like this guy, I decided it was time for me to move on. Flying back home that night, I felt a sense of relief and cleansing. I had been contemplating a career move into the training and consulting field. The huge mismatch between John's values and mine gave me the push I needed to take a new look at what was important to me in life and rethink my career direction. A few months later I joined forces with Art McNeil to build The Achieve Group (it became Canada's largest training and consulting firm over the next decade). Later I heard that many of John's leadership chickens (or perhaps turkeys) came home to roost. He was fired.

Worthwhile work

- More than half of the 2,300 respondents we surveyed at 50 top business schools were willing to take a 10-percent or greater salary reduction to work at a company that had values consistent with their own.

- When second-year students were asked to choose among 10 criteria for job selection, the overall choice was "values that are similar to mine" (number one with women; number two with men, after financial compensation).

- After graduation, women wanted to ensure they had meaningful work. Men sought learning and financial rewards. Ten years later women were looking for balance and fulfillment outside work (translation: time with family), whereas the men now badly wanted meaningful work.

The value of Values

My files continue to fill with studies that show the benefits of values-based leadership. Here are a few examples:

- A Boston College study examined the eight-year performance of 30 "socially conscious" companies. Those companies performed 106% better than their peer group.

- The Vermont-based Center for Economic Revitalization selected firms based on contributions to quality of life, responsible employee/labor relations, community participation, public service programs, and ethics. The "good guys" did indeed finish first. Over the 10-year period of the study, their share prices rose by 240%, while the Dow Jones Index increased by only 55%.

- Consultant and former Harvard professor David Maister surveyed employees at 139 worldwide offices of a large, diversified services firm. He found that employee attitudes and financial performance were closely correlated. The nine values leading to higher financial performance were: "client satisfaction is a top priority," "clients and the organization are put ahead of personal agendas," "higher performers get higher rewards," "management gets the best work from everyone," "high expectations for continuous skill development," "investing significant time in things that pay off in the future," "treating others with respect," "high quality of supervision," and "high quality of professional expertise."

- “Companies that spend money to develop and enforce a code of ethics will outperform their competitors,” according to a report entitled “Round Table on Public and Private Sector Ethics,” produced by the Conference Board of Canada for Public Works and Government Services Canada. “One recent study found a company’s overall performance is closely tied to its commitment to develop an ethical corporate culture,” the report says, referring to a study from DePaul University School of Accountancy. “Organizations making a public ethical commitment supported by senior management regularly outperform those that don’t.”

Profitability is a result, not a goal in itself. All else being equal, purposeful organizations are more profitable.

PURPOSE

"An organization without human commitment is like a person without a soul: Skeleton, flesh, and blood may be able to consume and to excrete, but there is no life force."

HENRY MINTZBERG, MANAGEMENT PROFESSOR AND AUTHOR

If the main reason for a company's existence is profit, it is often not very profitable. When a company is fixated with the bottom line, there's a good chance it won't survive. The dollar sign isn't a cause. It doesn't stir the soul. Operating margins and return on investment don't excite and inspire. As an ultimate objective on its own, the pursuit of profits is hollow and unsatisfying. It is one-dimensional, without depth. It comes from, and leads to, the naked selfishness of "what's in it for me."

Few people today want to buy from, work for, or partner with, a company that's only out for itself. For example, I can't imagine sitting down with my team, producing a set of elaborate architectural drawings for a huge, luxurious dream home, and saying, "if you all work really hard, someday this will be mine."

In his book *The Hungry Spirit: Beyond Capitalism – A Quest for Purpose in the Modern World,* Charles Handy writes, "The late David Packard, co-founder and inspiration of Hewlett Packard, one of the world's most respected international businesses, put it this way, shortly before he died: 'Why are we here? I think many people assume, wrongly, that a company exists solely to make money. Money is an important part of a company's existence, if the company is any good. But a result is not a cause. We have to go deeper and find the real reason for our being. As we investigate this, we inevitably come to the conclusion that a group of people get together and exist as an institution that we call a company, so that they are able to accomplish something collectively that they could not accomplish separately – they make a contribution to society, a phrase which sounds trite but is fundamental.'"

Writing in *Fortune* magazine, Geoffrey Colvin notes, "One trend in business is that employees, especially young employees, want a sense of purpose in their work. We all want a sense of purpose in our lives, but in the past we didn't demand it from our jobs. Now workers increasingly do. They want to know that what they do at work is good and right in some large sense."

Of course, if a company isn't profitable and financially strong, it won't exist long enough to serve any other purpose. That's the paradox to be managed: Companies that exist only to produce a profit don't last long, while companies that don't pay attention to profits can't exist to fulfill their long-term purpose. I call this the Profit Paradox. The key is to find the right middle ground, because pursuing profits without a higher purpose, or pursuing a purpose without profit, are equally fatal strategies.

Studies of the role and impact of values or ethics on corporate performance show that profits follow from worthy and useful purposes. Fulfilling the purpose comes first, and then the profits follow. Profits are a reward. The size of our reward depends on the value of the service we've given others.

Developing a purpose that's aimed at serving others adds a richer sense of meaning to our lives. It taps into the deep craving we all have to make a difference. We need to feel that the world was in some way a little bit better off for the brief time we passed through it.

FROM VICTIM TO VICTOR

Leaders don't blame others when things get tough. They recognize what can be done, what needs to be done, and they take charge of doing it.

RESPONSIBILITY FOR CHOICES

There are two kinds of people in the world: those who make excuses and those who get results. An excuse person will find any excuse for why a job was not done, and a results person will find any reason why it can be done. Be a creator, not a reactor.

ALAN COHEN, LEADERSHIP AUTHOR

No more excuses

"This is the excellent foppery of the world: that when we are sick in fortune – often the surfeits of our own behavior – we make guilty of our disasters the sun, the moon, and stars, as if we were villains on necessity, fools by heavenly compulsion, knaves, thieves, and treachers by spherical predominance, drunkards, liars, and adulterers by an enforced obedience of planetary influence. . . . An admirable evasion of whoremaster man, to lay his goatish disposition on the charge of a star!"

WILLIAM SHAKESPEARE, *KING LEAR*

When our son Chris was four years old he desperately wanted to graduate from his Big Wheel tricycle to a real two-wheeled bike. He started with training wheels on the bike but soon wanted them removed and didn't want me holding the bike for him. The result was that each time he tried to ride the bike, he'd fall after going just a short distance. After his sixth failed attempt, his frustration got the better of him: He grabbed the bike off the ground and bit the front tire as hard as he could. Clearly, it was all the bike's fault!

Part of me was right there with Chris biting the tire on that uncooperative bicycle. I can remember doing many similar things as a kid when I gave in to my hot temper. At family reunions, my uncle always liked to reminisce about the time, many years ago, when we had an old tractor that wouldn't run without stalling. His farm was next to ours and one day, noticing that the tractor and I hadn't moved for a long time, he drove back into our field to find out why. When he arrived he found the tractor covered in blotches of dirt from me angrily flinging clumps of soil at it.

We were having a lively discussion in a management workshop about the prevalence of "blame storming" in many organizations. The problem, we agreed, was that instead of tackling the problem, poorly led teams devote their energies to allocating blame and avoiding responsibility.

Of course, that's not leadership. One workshop participant wonderfully illustrated our all-too-human tendency to blame others by telling us about his four-year-old grandson's recent visit. Little Tim was the only visitor in the house that night. The next morning he came downstairs full of indignation. When asked what was wrong, he announced, "Somebody peed in my bed!"

It's natural to strike out at someone or something that seems to be causing us problems. We can understand this reaction in kids. After all, they're immature and still learning. They don't yet control much of their own lives. They aren't responsible for the circumstances in which they find themselves.

But as adults, we don't have the same excuses. We have to take responsibility for our choices. And we have to take responsibility for how we act in response to circumstances – even if those circumstances are not of our own making. This is the real test of our maturity and emotional intelligence. This is the "ground zero" of leadership.

Some things are beyond our control; others are not. Leaders understand the difference.

The Possibilities of Change

Your life is the sum result of all the choices you make, both consciously and unconsciously. If you can control the process of choosing, you can take control of all aspects of your life. You can find the freedom that comes from being in charge of yourself.

Robert Bennett, U.S. Senator

Accepting responsibility for choices starts with understanding where our choices lie. This idea is wonderfully framed by the timeless wisdom of the ancient Serenity Prayer:

God, grant me the serenity to accept the things
I cannot change,
The courage to change the things I can,
And the wisdom to know the difference.

Each line represents an important step in growing our leadership. Consider the first – an invocation to "grant me the serenity to accept the things I cannot change."

There is a long list of things we as leaders can't control, but may have a major impact on our organizations. These include economic and political trends, technological changes, shifts in consumer preferences and market trends, as well as catastrophes wrought by human beings (war, terrorism) and so-called "Acts of God," such as hurricanes or tornadoes. The poet Longfellow offers great leadership counsel about how to handle these non-controllables when he says, "the best thing one can do when it is raining is to let it rain." Pretty solid advice!

The fact is that stuff happens. Life isn't fair. Whatever hits the fan certainly won't be evenly distributed. The best approach to dealing with things that cannot be changed is to accept them. The worst thing we can do is to succumb to the Victimitis Virus and "awfulize" the situation by throwing pity parties in Pity City. When the doo-doo starts to pile deep, a leader doesn't just sit there and complain (usually about "them"); he or she grabs a shovel. We may not choose what happens to us, but we do choose how to respond – or not.

The second line of the Serenity Prayer asks for "the courage to change the things I can." This is the gulp-and-swallow part. Choosing to make changes is hard. It's so much easier to blame everyone else for my problems and to use this as an excuse for doing nothing. But leaders don't give away their power to choose. In his bestseller, *The Road Less Traveled*, Scott Peck writes, "Whenever we seek to avoid the responsibility for our own behavior, we do so by attempting to give that responsibility to some other individual or organization or entity. But this means we then give away our power to that entity, be it 'fate' or 'society' or the government or the corporation or our boss. It is for this reason that Erich Fromm so aptly titled his study of Nazism and authoritarianism, *Escape from Freedom*. In attempting to avoid the pain of responsibility, millions and even billions daily attempt to escape from freedom."

It takes real courage to accept full responsibility for our choices – especially for own attitude and outlook. This is the beginning and ultimately most difficult act of leadership.

The concluding line of the Serenity Prayer – "and the wisdom to know the difference" – is perhaps the toughest part of all. In our workshops with management teams we often get into lively debates about those things over which the group has the power to act. We attempt to classify them as belonging to three categories: No Control; Direct Control; and Influence. It's rarely black and white. For example, we often underestimate the influence we might have in our organizations – or in the world at large. But as Robert Kennedy once put it, "Each time a man stands up for an idea, or acts to improve the lot of others, or strikes out against injustice, he sends forth a tiny ripple of hope, and crossing each other from a million different centers of energy and daring, those ripples build a current that can sweep down the mightiest walls of oppression and resistance."

We're either part of the problem or part of the solution. There is no neutral ground. Strong leaders make the choice to be part of the solution and get on with it – no matter how small their ripples of change may be.

Steering the course

A Wagoner was once driving a heavy load along a very muddy way. At last he came to a part of the road where the wheels sank half-way into the mire, and the more the horses pulled, the deeper sank the wheels. So the Wagoner threw down his whip, and knelt down and prayed to Hercules the Strong. "O Hercules, help me in this my hour of distress." Hercules appeared to him, and said: "Tut, man, don't sprawl there. Get up and put your shoulder to the wheel."

AESOP, FROM THE FABLE "FATE HELPS THEM THAT HELP THEMSELVES"

The three P's of pessimism

Psychologist Martin Seligman has found that pessimists fall into the trap of the three Ps when faced with a negative change or setback. They make the issue Permanent, Pervasive and Personal. They avoid wearing clean underwear because it will only tempt car accidents. These victims adhere to their own kind of "Anti-Serenity Prayer":

God, grant me the anxiety to try to control the things I cannot control,

The fear to avoid the things I can,

And the neurosis to deny the difference.

When faced with difficult change or problems, we have three choices. We can be a Survivor and just hang in there, hoping for the best, sitting on the fence, and waiting to see what happens. Or we can choose to be a Victim, using the situation as one more example of how these terrible things keep happening to us.

The third choice – the leadership choice – is to be a Navigator and trim our sails or steer our boat to get through the storm and continue on to our preferred future. Navigators know that we're constantly faced by great opportunities brilliantly disguised as unsolvable problems. Too often we wait for someone to open the door when the handle is actually on the inside.

Navigators choose to make things happen. Survivors watch things happen. Victims complain bitterly that "this crap is always happening to me."

Accentuate the positive

"The ripple effect of a leader's enthusiasm and optimism is awesome. So is the impact of cynicism and pessimism. Leaders who whine and blame engender those same behaviors among their colleagues. I am not talking about stoically accepting organizational stupidity and performance incompetence with a "what, me worry?" smile. I am talking about a gung-ho attitude that says 'we can change things here, we can achieve awesome goals, we can be the best.' Spare me the grim litany of the 'realist,' give me the unrealistic aspirations of the optimist any day."

COLIN POWELL, U.S. SECRETARY OF STATE

Just as pessimism erodes our ability to deal successfully with change, so does optimism enhance it. Consider what some of the experts have found.

- From Daniel Goleman, Richard Boyatzis and Annie McKee, writing in *Primal Leadership: Realizing the Power of Emotional Intelligence*: "No one wants to work for a grouch. Research has proven it: Optimistic, enthusiastic leaders more easily retain their people, compared with those bosses who tend toward negative moods...numerous studies show that when the leader is in a happy mood, the people around him view everything in a more positive light. That, in turn, makes them optimistic about achieving their goals, enhances their creativity and the efficiency of their decision making, and predisposes them to be helpful."

- A University of Michigan study of 70 work teams found that within two hours people in meetings ended up sharing good or bad moods.
- From Martin Seligman, in *Learned Optimism*: "Learned helplessness is the giving-up reaction, the quitting response that follows from the belief that whatever you do doesn't matter. Explanatory style is the manner in which you habitually explain to yourself why events happen.... An optimistic explanatory style stops helplessness, whereas a pessimistic explanatory style spreads helplessness."

A father was late getting to his son's baseball game. As he sat down behind the players' bench he asked one of the boys known as a real leader on the team what the score was.

"We're behind 14 to nothing," he answered with a smile.

"Really!" the Dad replied. "I am surprised that you don't look very discouraged." "Discouraged?" the boy replied with a puzzled look on his face. "Why should we be discouraged? We haven''t been up to bat yet."

Optimism

Talk happiness. The world is sad enough
Without your woes. No path is wholly rough;
Look for the places that are smooth and clear,
And speak of those, to rest the weary ear
Of Earth, so hurt by one continuous strain
Of human discontent and grief and pain.

Talk faith. The world is better off without
Your uttered ignorance and morbid doubt.
If you have faith in God, or man, or self,
Say so. If not, push back upon the shelf
Of silence all your thoughts, till faith shall come;
No one will grieve because your lips are dumb.

Talk health. The dreary, never-changing tale
Of mortal maladies is worn and stale.
You cannot charm, or interest, or please
By harping on that minor chord, disease.
Say you are well, or all is well with you,
And God shall hear your words and make them true.

Ella Wheeler Wilcox

Most barriers to our leadership are self-imposed.

PRISONS OF THE MIND

Everything can be taken from a man but one thing: the last of the human freedoms – to choose one's attitude in any given set of circumstances, to choose one's own way. And there were always choices to make. Every day, every hour, offered the opportunity to make a decision, a decision which determined whether you would or would not submit to those powers which threatened to rob you of your very self, your inner freedom; which determined whether or not you would become the plaything of circumstance, renouncing freedom and dignity to become molded into the form of the typical inmate.

VIKTOR FRANKL, *MAN'S SEARCH FOR MEANING: EXPERIENCES IN THE CONCENTRATION CAMP*

W Mitchell is an outstanding example of someone who refuses to be a victim, despite being victimized – not by just one horrible accident, but two. The first left him burned over 65% of his body, including his face, arms, and hands. A plane crash four years later left him paralyzed from the waist down, sentencing him permanently to a wheelchair. Having overcome these setbacks, Mitchell is a very compelling speaker on taking responsibility for our choices in life – on what it takes to be a leader.

One of Mitchell's speaking sessions typically begins with an introduction, after which he rolls out on stage in his wheelchair, looks out over the audience and asks if any of them has ever been in prison. Silence. He then goes on to declare that he's been in prison and it was horrible. At this point the members of the audience begin to look at one another and wonder if some details of his past were conveniently omitted during his introduction. Is this guy a felon or what? Mitchell then goes on to talk about self-imposed "mental wheelchairs" that hold so many people back from being highly effective leaders.

"I firmly believe that most barriers are self-imposed," Mitchell writes in *It's Not What Happens to You, It's What You Do About It*. "We first get them from society – you can't do that, that's immoral, that's crazy, no one in our family does that, and so on – but we forget that we have the power to accept or reject these barriers. We treat them as if they are immovable, immutable, when, in fact, they may be silly, cause unnecessary misery, or just be plain nonexistent."

Mitchell delivers a powerful leadership message in his speeches. But his most powerful message can be found in the example of his life. Mitchell takes full responsibility for his choices in response to circumstances for which he is not responsible. "Nothing, absolutely nothing is absolute," he says. "Your life is entirely what you decide it is... The universe starts in your head and spreads out into the world. Change what happens in your head, and the universe changes." (You can visit his website at www.wmitchell.com for more information on this remarkable leader.)

Monkey see, monkey do

Many experiments are done with monkeys, especially rhesus monkeys, which closely resemble the human animal – not just physically but, it seems, psychologically as well. Here we see compelling evidence of the all-too-human tendency to make assumptions based not on our own experience, but on the attitudes of others.

In one experiment, researchers placed a number of rhesus monkeys into a specially designed room. Once a day the researchers would lower a bunch of nice fresh bananas, as a treat to supplement their regular food, through a hole in the ceiling. However, when the monkeys would grab one of the bananas, they were subjected to a blast of cold air, with the result that they would drop the bananas and scurry quickly away. After a few days of this, the monkeys would not even go near the bananas. Even after the cold-air mechanism was turned off, they refused to risk any further attempt to get the bananas.

Then the researchers began to change the makeup of the group. Every day, they removed one monkey from the room and replaced it with a new monkey who had never experienced the cold blast of air. Not surprisingly, the original members of the group continued to avoid the bananas. What was most interesting, however, was that the newly introduced monkeys also avoided them. Even after the researchers had replaced all the monkeys so that none had ever experienced the blast of cold air, not a single monkey in the room would go near the bananas.

Adapted from Luke De Sadeleer and Joseph Sherren, *Vitamin C for a Healthy Workplace*

Management without limits

"If you don't change your beliefs, your life will be like this forever. Is that good news?"

– Douglas Adams, British author of *A Hitchhiker's Guide to the Galaxy*

Head-office "wheelchairs"

I was doing an assessment and planning retreat with one of the divisions of a large multinational company. The team was bitter about the limitations their head office placed upon them. They felt that their IT system severely restricted what their division could do. They thought that many rules and policies boxed them in too tightly. They all agreed that there was never enough money to invest what was really needed to move the company forward. Many times when I or another group member would give an improvement suggestion, somebody else would shoot it down with a snicker, snide bit of humor, or a comment like "New York [their head office] would never go for that."

Clearly, this team's lack of leadership was paralyzing the division and frustrating most people there. So I told them the story of W Mitchell (see page 63). We talked about "mental wheelchairs," leadership, and taking control of our situations. We discussed some aspects of head office they could try to influence. However, as a small division in a large company, they would have to live with many of the head office limitations. This was their wheelchair.

Unlike Mitchell, each person there had a choice; they could remain in the company and lead from their wheelchair or they could leave and go somewhere else. They finally agreed that as long as they remained in the company in a management role, they had an obligation to provide positive leadership around the things that they could control or influence, while letting go of those things they could not control.

An unhealthy lack of leadership

During another retreat with the management team of a large hospital, we were running a little behind schedule so I said we'd move fairly quickly through the Responsibility for Choices principle in our leadership discussion. Fortunately, a more astute participant piped up with, "Jim, I think we need to talk about how often we blame everyone else for our problems and give up trying to solve them. We blame the unions, the physicians, our board, those paying the bills, the patients and their families, other agencies, the government, and so on. I think we're disempowering ourselves and failing to provide leadership to our teams." He was absolutely right. We went on to a very productive discussion about their "blaming and disclaiming" culture and what this team of leaders could do to reverse that.

Political "blame storming"

The management team for a large municipality was very angry about the new council that had just been elected and would be with them for next two years. The council had been elected on a platform of major reform and was micromanaging by getting into all kinds of details as they made a number of big changes to the municipality's operations, services, and costs. The workshop conversation was all about how council wouldn't let management do their jobs. Whenever new ideas for change and improvement emerged, someone would bitterly scoff at it and point out that council would never support it. The conversation often drifted into the larger realm of the stupidity of political interference and how difficult it was to manage in an environment where the media was constantly prowling for examples of inept management that would reinforce negative public perceptions.

We then talked about examples of people who had become outstanding leaders despite major obstacles. We discussed people like W Mitchell (see page 63), Alvin Law (a very successful speaker who was born without arms; you can read his remarkable story at www.alvinlaw.com), or Carl Hiebert (a professional photographer, author, and philanthropist to Third World causes who lost the use of his legs in a hang-gliding accident; read about him at www.carlhiebert.com). We talked about how cynicism isn't leadership. Leaders bring hope and possibilities. We discussed how leaders take responsibility in reacting to circumstances for which they are not responsible. We looked at how much easier it is to point fingers or throw up our hands and quit trying until "they" get their act together. We talked about how life in government organizations is full of maddening political interference. But, hey, it's called democracy. Would anyone in the room prefer the alternative?

As we progressed in our discussions, the group began to change its tone and started to talk about what could be. We began sorting out what could be controlled, couldn't be controlled, and what could be influenced. They brainstormed, clustered ideas together, set priorities, debated alternatives, and set action plans. They got on with it. Two years later, acting on these plans, they had made huge strides forward in changing and improving their organization despite the obstacles, handicaps, and problems. It's called leadership.

No matter where you are in the organizational hierarchy, it's essential to be a leader. Often that calls for upward leadership.

I'M IN CHARGE

Don't curse the darkness, light a candle.
CHINESE PROVERB

In our leadership workshops most team leaders, supervisors, and middle managers agree wholeheartedly that far too many people in their organization succumb to the Victimitis virus – the poor-little-me syndrome. This tendency is often revealed by statements like "they are doing it to me again," "there's nothing I can do," or "it's all their fault." Looking right past themselves, these managers then look for ways to change everyone else.

Too often managers don't recognize the extent of their own Victimitis. They aspire to lead but end up demoralizing their own teams and frustrate themselves by choosing to be disempowered by their boss or others above them in the organization. They give away their power by believing that they don't have any. They unwittingly become proponents of "heroic management" – the belief that leadership only comes down from the top.

That's a real shame, because these potential "middle leaders" could have a real impact on their own teams or on their part of the organization. Instead they become models of helplessness and cynicism. They often complain bitterly as they wait for their boss and others higher in the organization to take action. It's all too easy to point a finger upward and shake our heads in disgust. It is much harder to point a finger in the mirror and see a potential source of our leadership problems.

Regardless of where they might be in the organizational hierarchy, strong leaders don't make the mistake of behaving as though they work for someone else. You won't find them saying, "They ought to do something about that." Instead, they'll say, "I will do something about that."

Robert Redford: The patient evolutionary

Since the 1980s, actor and director Robert Redford has led a quiet revolution to change the entire movie industry by opening it up to artistic diversity. His Utah-based Sundance Institute has become one of the most influential forces in Hollywood – incubating independent films that break new cinematic ground. As a profile of Redford in the *Harvard Business Review* noted, "His multi-faceted approach to change includes developing grassroots initiatives; earning credibility and then leveraging his successes; practicing the art of compromise and persuasion in order to get projects accomplished; gathering support along the way; and, most important, demonstrating persistence."

Movie stars aren't usually perceptive sources of leadership insight! But Redford's reflections on decades of patient and successful leadership from the inside-out provide a very useful lesson on how to lead an evolution as an "outside-insider":

"A better way to change a system is to work through it as a bottom-up insider, quietly chipping away at standard operating procedures, creating small opportunities to do what you really want to do, until you achieve a real success. Then you can break out your agenda in a larger way."

"I learned that the corporate powers that be aren't going to be interested in the fruits of your labor and passion unless you are adept at understanding their agenda and speaking their language... You can't be forceful, loud, confrontational, or declarative. You have to sell what you have on their terms."

"Once you have earned credibility and are in a position to get what you want, you need to strike a series of devil's bargains. To horse-trade with the devil, you have to look him squarely in the eye and make the right demands from him."

"I concluded that if you want to crack the system, you can't hit it directly; you have to work behind the scenes."

Leading from the middle

"Good leaders don't wait for official blessing to try things out. Less effective middle managers endorsed the sentiment, 'If I haven't explicitly been told yes I can't do it,' whereas the good ones believed, 'If I haven't explicitly been told no, I can.' There's a world of difference between these two points of view."

Colin Powell, U.S. Secretary of State

We work with many middle managers – people with titles such as department head, branch manager, or director. They are truly sandwiched in the middle between executives, who develop strategy and long-term goals, and first-level supervisors or frontline team leaders, who manage day-to-day operations. Middle managers end up being promoted to their positions for a variety of reasons that often don't include proven leadership ability. These reasons might include significant technical expertise, effectiveness in managing processes and systems, generally solid performance, dependability, being in the right place at the right time as the organization went through rapid growth, or being especially astute political players.

Middle managers have been derided as dinosaurs. I've heard more than one executive team express frustration about "middle management mush" as they tried to implement their strategies or bring about organizational change. Efforts at "flattening" organizations often involve trying to remove layers of middle management.

There is a difference between middle managers and middle leaders. Both are needed. However, most organizations need stronger leadership to counterbalance years of focus on management systems, processes, and technology. The best middle leaders provide strong leadership up, down, and across the organization. They use influence, persuasion, "tempered radicalism" (see page 78), networking, and other skills to lead at the speed of change.

Research indicates that effective middle leaders make valuable contributions to change in successful organizations. INSEAD professor Quy Nguyen Huy found that strong middle leaders have good entrepreneurial ideas. They are often better than executives at leveraging informal networks. The best ones stayed attuned to and meet the emotional needs of people throughout the organization during major change. Effective middle leaders also manage the ongoing tension between continuity and change.

Making the best of a bad boss

"…. At one point, I had an extraordinarily difficult boss, who could literally drive you into tears. And it was easy to convince yourself to allow the fear that naturally arose to, if not paralyze you, certainly greatly restrict what you did, and the risks you were willing to take. And I think coming to grips with that was not an easy one…I decided life was too short to hide in the corner and worry about this guy. And I also decided that I was right, and he wasn't."

JOHN KOTTER, LEADERSHIP AUTHOR AND HARVARD BUSINESS SCHOOL PROFESSOR

Strong leaders don't allow themselves to be victims of a bad boss. Choosing to do that is like choosing to hang wallpaper with one arm tied behind our back. Many managers lose the "boss lottery" and, through no fault of their own, end up reporting to an ineffective executive. We may not be able to choose our boss, but we can choose how to respond to him or her. Good leaders refuse to be a victim of their boss's weaknesses. They don't let a dumb boss make them act dumb. They know that the worst thing they can do is to sabotage their careers just to spite the boss.

Unless the boss is so bad that a bigger career decision (i.e. looking for a new job) is called for, a strong leader tries to make the best of a difficult situation. What can I learn from this boss? Sometimes a bad example – of what not to do and how not to behave – is very instructive! Keep in mind, too, that your boss may not be as entirely bad as you might think. Ask yourself: What are the boss's strengths that I could learn from? Am I allowing my own style or preferences to cloud my opinion and damage our relationship? For example, is he or she cold and analytical while I am more emotional and focused on people – or vice versa? (Typically the people we have the most problems with are those at the opposite end of our own behavioral style.)

Ask yourself, too, whether there are ways you can play to your boss's strengths and preferences. Are there other people reporting to your boss who have a good relationship with him or her? If so, and assuming that these people aren't simply sucking up to the boss, can I emulate some of what they are doing to build a better relationship with the boss? Do I know what work issues are keeping my boss awake at night? Can I link the changes I am trying to lead to those "hot button" issues? Could I more effectively partner with my boss to use his or her higher organizational position to leverage the larger change or leadership agenda I am trying to drive forward? Do I understand the bigger political picture of which my boss is a part? Am I "stage managing" my boss to help him or her look good and bring the additional weight of his or her office to our situations?

Many bad bosses do a poor job of planning, setting priorities, and following through. Sometimes that's because he or she is being pulled in many directions by forces beyond his or her control. Do I know what those are? Other times bosses are just disorganized and undisciplined. But before I throw a Pity Party and complain about that, I need to take a look in the mirror. How's my leadership example? Strong leaders take the initiative to regularly plan, set priorities, and follow through with his or her boss. Does my boss share the same sense of urgency I have about the changes that need to be made in our organization? Have I done enough to increase his or her understanding of the need for change?

Leadership is action, not a position.

JUST GO AND DO IT

The world bestows its big prizes both in money and honors for but one thing. And that is initiative. And what is initiative? I'll tell you: it is doing the right thing without being told.

ELBERT HUBBARD, AMERICAN EDITOR, PUBLISHER, AND AUTHOR

Don't wait – initiate! That's the deeply embedded belief system of strong leaders. An ancient Chinese proverb teaches that "the person who waits for a roast duck to fly into their mouth must wait a very long time." Regardless of their position or role, leaders don't wait for something to happen or someone to tell them what to do. They go and do it.

We often refer to leadership as a position. Because someone has been appointed to a leadership role they are called a leader. But many people in leadership roles aren't leaders. They might be vice presidents, CEOs, managers, administrators, department heads, directors, or "snoopervisors" – but they're not leaders. They aren't leaders because they sit back and wait or become victims rather than taking initiative and making things happen. In other words, they don't provide leadership through their actions.

In his book *Getting Things Done When You're Not in Charge*, Geoffrey Bellman writes about "familiar and disempowering words like 'If our team leader would just tell us what he really expects of us,' 'The Board just won't say what they want done!' or 'If she would just tell us, we'd be glad to do it!'" He goes on to advise, "Do not wait to be called upon... Our only chance for contributing is to quit waiting and wondering and do something. We serve ourselves and others best when we do not wait. Initiate, with the organization and all involved people in mind. No, we are not in charge, but we can act. No, we are not formally designated leaders. But we can lead."

Leadership researcher, author, and Harvard Business School professor John Kotter strongly asserts that "leaders must understand that leadership is not just a job of the person above them in the hierarchy... the most common sort of leadership that you see today that is useful are people who challenge the status quo, vacuum up information from all directions, establish – by themselves or with others – a sense of direction, vision, for their little piece of the action, and then create some strategies for making the vision a reality."

Tempered radicals: Steely leadership choices

"Tempered radicals lead through inspiration. They inspire change and they inspire other people, not through daring acts of courage, but through their ability to keep going, to tough it out, and to rise above their own frustration, humiliation, and anger to act on behalf of their larger ideals."

Debra Meyerson, a professor of organizational behavior at Stanford, conducted in-depth interviews with almost 200 successful "tempered radicals" in three very different organizations. (The term "tempered radicals" describes those change-leaders who use their anger or energy to alternatively heat and cool their approaches as they become tougher and stronger. This is the same tempering process that strengthens steel.) She was looking for the ways these leaders effect change, while staying true to themselves. She also studied how they leveraged small wins, and organized collective action.

Meyerson's book, *Tempered Radicals: How People Use Difference to Inspire Change at Work*, provides powerful guidance about how to lead from persuasion and persistence rather than from "position power." It is all about harnessing or tempering frustration and using it to lead.

- *"Tempered Radicals are people who want to succeed in their organizations yet want to live by their values or identities, even if they are somehow at odds with the dominant culture of their organizations. Tempered radicals want to fit in and they want to retain what makes them different. They want to rock the boat, and they want to stay in it."*
- *"Tempered radicals are people who operate on a fault line. They are organizational insiders who contribute and succeed in their jobs. At the same time, they are treated as outsiders because they represent ideals or agendas that are somehow at odds with the dominant culture."*
- *"Tempered radicals may believe in questioning fundamental principles (e.g., how to allocate resources) or root assumptions, but they do not advocate extreme measures. They work within systems, not against them."*
- *"They inspire by having courage to tell the truth even when it's difficult to do so, and by having the conviction to stay engaged in tough conversations. They inspire by demonstrating the commitment to stay focused on their larger ideals even when they suffer consequences or get little recognition for doing so. Their leadership does not rely on inspiring through periodic heroism and headlines. Their leadership inspires – and matters – in big and small ways every day."*
- *"It is leadership that tends to be less visible, less coordinated, and less vested with formal authority; it is also more local, more diffuse, more opportunistic, and more humble than the activity attributed to the modern-day hero. This version of leadership depends not on charismatic flair, instant success, or inspirational visions, but on qualities such as patience, self-knowledge, humility, flexibility, idealism, vigilance, and commitment."*

LET'S GET REAL

Noble intentions and inspiring words are all very important. But we can't lead other people to become something that we are not ourselves.

AUTHENTICITY

In the end, it's the quality and character of the leader that determines an organization's performance and results. Think about this in relation to the job of transmitting the organization's values. It's not enough for the leader just to say, 'There are our values.' If those values are really going to permeate the organization, the leader has to embody them. The army has a wonderful shorthand. They say, 'Be, know, do.' I believe that any discussion of leadership has to begin with how to be.

FRANCES HESSELBEIN, CHAIR OF THE PETER F. DRUCKER FOUNDATION

We all know that strong leaders are the real deal. They embody the leadership clichés like "walk the talk" or "lead by example." Strong leaders maintain a close connection between what they say and what they do. Their video is in sync with their audio. The vision (and values and purpose) they set out for their team or organization is no different from what they set out for their own lives. Leaders don't try to make others into something that they are not themselves.

Know thyself

A Penn State survey found that managers who are well aware of their leadership style are more likely to succeed at their jobs than their peers. The study's author, John Sasik, associate professor of management and organization, concludes, "Leaders need to be aware of the way they present themselves to their followers. Self-aware managers tend to be the best performers because they are able to change their behavior and adapt to changes in the organizational environment, whether that's new technology, working with people from different cultures or leading new business initiatives."

"When Thales was asked what was difficult, he said, 'To know one's self.' And what was easy, 'To advise another.'"

DIOGENES, GREEK PHILOSOPHER, 412 - 323 B.C.

"The first piece of advice we give to people who come to GE's management training center in Crotonville, NY is, 'Get to know your own style.' We try to help each person discover how he or she is most effective as a leader.... whatever their styles, we can show them the kinds of meetings and review processes that play to their advantages."

CYNTHIA TRAGGE-LAKRA, MANAGER OF EXECUTIVE DEVELOPMENT, GENERAL ELECTRIC

"Emotional Awareness: Recognizing one's emotions and their effects. People with this competence:

- Know which emotions they are feeling and why;
- Realize the links between their feelings and what they think, do, and say;
- Recognize how their feelings affect their performance;
- Have a guiding awareness of their values and goals."

THE FIRST OF FOUR COMPONENTS OF THE EMOTIONAL COMPETENCE FRAMEWORK, POSTED AT THE WEBSITE FOR THE CONSORTIUM FOR REACH ON EMOTIONAL INTELLIGENCE IN ORGANIZATIONS.

Authentic leaders build the trust that bridges the gaps between "us and them." Such leaders have high integrity and consistency. They foster environments of openness and transparency, which gets real issues on the table. Their personal authenticity encourages authentic conversations that pull the team together. As a result, teams get to the heart of performance issues rather than playing politics or sucking up to the boss.

Authenticity isn't something you can fake – although we all know managers who think they can get ahead by doing so. These wannabe leaders are like Groucho Marx who declared, "I've got strong values. I am going to stand tough on those values. And if you don't like those values... I've got others."

In today's increasingly skeptical (and, some might say, cynical) society, our BS detectors are getting much better at exposing these leadership fakes. Such people are routinely exposed through various media – in television reports, books, newspapers, even by cartoon characters (like the pointy-haired Dilbert boss). They are revealed as "empty suits" who aren't authentic leaders at all.

What's worse is that whenever an inauthentic leader is exposed, it adds to people's suspicion of all leaders – fake and genuine alike. This is a persistent challenge for all those who aspire to grow their leadership, and makes the role of authenticity particularly vital.

Authentic leaders look deep within to understand their real vision, values, and purpose.

Being True to Me

Be brave enough to live creatively. The creative is the place where no one else has ever been. You have to leave the city of your comfort and go into the wilderness of your intuition. You cannot get there by bus, only by hard work, risking and by not quite knowing what you are doing. What you will discover will be wonderful; yourself.

Alan Alda, actor, writer, and director

I once heard ballet dancer Karen Kain reflecting on how lucky she felt to have become a dancer, since it was this life's work that had allowed her to "find her voice" – to express what was truly inside herself.

Miles Dewey Davis, Jr. has been called "the Picasso of Jazz" for his creativity and constant reinvention of his music. He was the forerunner and innovator of many distinct and important musical movements. As Davis once noted, "Sometimes you have to play for a long time to play like yourself."

"Finding my voice" is a phrase often used by artists, writers, musicians, and other creative people to describe the (often difficult) process of learning from other artists' styles and, from these, developing the style that most truly represents yourself. This applies not just to artists, but to people in just about any walk of life. Each of us learns from what surrounds us – for example, the expectations and value systems of parents, society, institutions, friends, peers, our boss, or our organization. But then we have to ask ourselves whether these things really reflect our own personal values. And if they don't, we need to move beyond them to find what does. This takes a lot of work – and even more courage.

One of the toughest times in my life was the two-year period after I had sold my interest in The Achieve Group to California-based Zenger Miller. I spent many sleepless nights and morning mediation and weekend reflection time trying to find a place for myself in the new company. I tried unsuccessfully numerous ways to influence the larger company in the direction I felt it needed to go. I felt like I was wandering in the proverbial desert without a clear role and direction that fit me.

Ultimately, I felt my only choice was to leave. In doing so I left behind a secure job and substantial salary for the uncertainty of independent speaking, workshops, and consulting in a new business we called The CLEMMER Group. In our first five years of business, Heather and I earned a combined annual income of less than half (sometimes less than a quarter) of what I would have made had I stayed with Zenger Miller (later merged with other training companies to become Achieve Global). And this was with substantially longer hours and harder work than before. Still, it was the right thing to do because I have always believed, like the late comedian George Burns, that "it is better to be a failure at something you love than to be a success at something you hate."

The guiding vision of my career has been less about where I want to go and more about who I want to become. There have been times when this has meant passing up lucrative opportunities because they didn't fit that vision. But I am even more convinced today that if we are to remain true to ourselves, we must always keep searching for what will fulfill our vision, values, and purpose.

Our values are most truly revealed when times are toughest. When the heat is on and the pressure is building, what do we care most about? Psychiatrist and author Elizabeth Kübler-Ross once provided this powerful observation: "People are like stained-glass windows. They sparkle and shine when the sun is out, but when the darkness sets in, their true beauty is revealed only if there is a light from within."

So what's my light within? Where is my energy source? How do I stay centered and focused when challenged with major, negative changes – when the need for strong leadership is greatest? As jazz great Charlie Parker once said, "Jazz comes from who you are, where you've been, what you've done. If you don't live it, it won't come out of your horn."

Consult the wisdom of the ages or the latest research studies and you'll always find that leadership is an inside job. Before I can *have*, I must *do*. Before I can *do*, I must *be*. This critical sequence of Be-Do-Have is at the center of authentic leadership. It all starts with *being* a leader.

Leaders can't please everyone

We spend much of our lives trying to please others: parents, spouses and other family members, as well as friends and colleagues. All these external influences can drown out our internal voice. We know intellectually that trying to please everybody is a recipe for disaster. But emotionally, it's a difficult habit to break. We instinctively want the approval of others.

"The boy rode on the donkey and the old man walked. As they went along they passed some people who remarked it was a shame the old man was walking and the boy was riding. The man and boy thought that maybe the critics were right, so they changed positions.

Later, they passed some people that remarked, 'What a shame, he makes that little boy walk.' They then decided they both would walk! Soon they passed some more people who thought they were stupid to walk when they had a decent donkey to ride. So, they both rode the donkey.

Now they passed some people that shamed them by saying how awful to put such a load on a poor donkey. The boy and man said they were probably right, so they decided to carry the donkey. As they crossed the bridge, they lost their grip on the animal and he fell into the river and drowned.

Moral: If you try to please everyone, you might as well kiss your ass good-bye."

MARK ALBION, AUTHOR OF *MAKING A LIFE, MAKING A LIVING*

Honesty and integrity create trust.
Trust builds confidence.
Confidence drives success.

Moral Authorities

> *The first step toward greatness is to be honest.*
>
> Samuel Johnson

Honesty and integrity are motherhood leadership phrases. And they should be. They are fundamental to leadership. Honesty and integrity produces trust, which produces high levels of confidence. High confidence encourages people to dream and to reach for new horizons. High confidence fosters risk-taking. Risk-taking and initiative are fundamental to organization change and improvement.

Our ability to lead others is directly related to our ability to forge strong relationships. Strong relationships are dependent upon trust. Trust provides the glue.

Surveys of people throughout many organizations are showing that about half of them admit to unethical business practices! No wonder so many organizations are suffering from a crisis of morale. Neither is it surprising that cynicism runs rampant and people feel an

Authenticity means integrity

The measure of a man's real character is what he would do if he knew he would never be found out.

Lord Thomas Macauley, 19th-century British historian

An applicant was filling out a job application. When he came to the question, "Have you ever been arrested?" he wrote, "No."

The next question, intended for people who had answered in the affirmative to the previous question, was "Why?"

The applicant answered it anyway: "Never got caught."

ever-diminishing commitment to their organizations. Clearly, this situation will not change without strong, trustworthy leadership at all levels. Rebuilding trust demands authentic leaders who are courageous enough not to become victims of their toxic cultures or their own unethical bosses.

Most managers agree that building trust is essential to an organization's success. Studies continually show that mistrust of management and low morale are significant factors in the widening we-they gap between frontline people and managers. A survey by The Discovery Group, a company specializing in employee opinion surveys, found that 52% of employees don't believe the information they receive from management.

Compounding the problem of declining trust among employees is that many managers don't seem to be aware of it. For example, a Lakewood Research study asked managers and employees to respond to the statement, "This company genuinely cares about the well-being and morale of the employees and takes action to help people feel good about working here." Two-thirds of managers agreed with the statement. However, less than one-fifth of their employees did!

Measuring the value of trust

A study of the eight biggest automobile manufacturers in Japan, South Korea, and the United States, along with 435 of their suppliers, looked at the economic value of trust (defined as "confidence that the other party will not exploit one's vulnerabilities"). "The results of [the] research indicated that in all three countries relationships with higher levels of trust had substantially lower costs. Trust actually adds value to the relationship because it encourages the sharing of resources."

A study commissioned by *Macleans* magazine found that companies whose employees believe their bosses are good people-managers are the ones with the strongest shareholder returns. "Where trust in management is high," says Dawn Bell, a Vancouver-based senior consultant with Watson Wyatt Worldwide, "it is incredible what employees can do to drive business success. In organizations where the trust and confidence has gone, it is very difficult just to keep the lights on."

All too often, managers expect frontline staff to know their place – and stay there.

'WE' AND 'THEY'

I could never believe that Providence had sent a few men into the world ready booted and spurred to ride, and millions ready saddled and bridled to be ridden.

SEVENTEENTH-CENTURY BRITISH SOLDIER RICHARD RUMBOLD'S FINAL WORDS ON THE SCAFFOLD BEFORE HE WAS HANGED. QUOTED BY THOMAS JEFFERSON IN HIS REFLECTIONS ON THE UNDERLYING PRINCIPLES IN THE AMERICAN DECLARATION OF INDEPENDENCE.

Ask any group of managers if they view themselves as an elite within their organization, and you can be sure they'll deny it. You'll hear comments such as, "I have an open-door policy" and "I take pride in always being accessible and approachable."

And in most cases, these managers will really believe what they are saying. What they don't realize, however, are the many invisible barriers – the "glass doors" – they put in place. Management perks and privileges like parking spaces or special offices create separation. Similarly, employees find it hard to get any sense of partnership or collaboration when their bosses hold exclusive meetings or conferences, hang out in management cliques, use condescending or dehumanizing language, or withhold financial statements or other "confidential" information.

Here again we see an example of what separates leaders from managers. Leaders put a real effort into listening to, and learning from, people throughout their organization. Listening is the clearest way we can show respect. Listening builds trust. By contrast, managers don't listen to "their people" – usually because they're too busy telling them what they need. Managers spend major amounts of time in their offices or in meetings with other managers and specialists. They often control and command by email because they see it as a more efficient use of their time. Occasionally they might do an organizational survey or hold a meeting or special event for "their people."

Money is good, respect is better

Labor lawyer Stuart Saxe runs workshops helping managers learn how they can stay union-free. He begins each session by asking managers to rank, in order of importance, what employees want. Money always heads the list. But when employees are asked the same question, "respect is at the top of the list," reports Saxe. "You have to understand that you can't be snobs. The employees who work for you consider their jobs as important as you think your job is," he tells the managers.

Libby Sartain, VP, People, and Jim Parker, CEO and Vice Chair of the Board at Southwest Airlines strongly agree: "Most labor disputes are not really about money. There is something else at stake – respect. It comes down to personal contact between the company and its employees. This is one reason our supervisors are so important. It is easier to walk out on people who do not give you respect than to walk out on a friend. And you cannot make up for longstanding problems in the two months before a negotiation. It needs to be consistent."

Strong leaders, on the other hand, have their own kind of "closed-door" policy. Not that they're trying to keep people out. It's just that most of the time you'll find their office doors closed and the lights off – because leaders are so rarely satisfied with staying behind a desk. Leaders know that an office is a dangerous place from which to manage an organization. Leaders also recognize that few of "their partners" (frontline people) are going to be assertive enough to break through the invisible management barriers to come into their office and raise an issue. Many aren't going to send an email. Studies show that in many organizations a majority of frontline people are afraid to speak up. That's why leaders spend huge amounts of time with people throughout their organization. They're busy listening at breakfasts, lunches, barbecues, and town hall meetings. They're conducting surveys, participating in cafeteria conversations, working together with people on the frontlines, and attending celebration events.

Leading in the rain

On a rainy day in 1943 a battalion was lined up waiting for an inspection by Lord Mountbatten. The officers wore raincoats, but the troops had none. They were soaked. Mountbatten's car pulled up and he emerged wearing a raincoat. After taking a few steps, he turned around and went back to the car to shed his raincoat. He then turned to make the inspection. The troops cheered.

Sharing tough times

It's when times are toughest that everyone most clearly sees authentic leadership. This is when much-repeated claims like "our people are our most important assets" ("leaderspeak") are proven true, or just so much hollow rhetoric. How managers handle economic downturns and sudden cost-reduction pressures, for example, speaks volumes about their leadership – or lack thereof. If an organization has strong leaders who truly care about people and want to build long-term trust, layoffs are always the very last, desperate step. Such leaders operate from core values of partnership and participation. They don't look at people within the organization as "heads," "FTEs (Full Time Equivalents)," "warm bodies," or faceless "human resources" to be acquired and disposed of like assets on a balance sheet.

Leading successfully in tough times calls for openness, a willingness to outline the difficult situation clearly, and provide cost-reduction guidelines, as well as an ability to express our own pain. Leaders use all the methods at their disposal – including surveys, meetings, email exchanges/polling, focus groups, town halls, and phone hotlines – to facilitate brainstorming, get input, set priorities, and make joint decisions and action plans. Then they communicate, communicate – and communicate some more. Leaders know that it's almost impossible to tell people too much about what's going on and why. "Over-communication" is rarely a source of poor morale and dissatisfaction. (Information overload, however, can be very demoralizing. A leader knows there's a

Thirsting for leadership

Alexander the Great was leading his forces across a scorching terrain. For 11 days they pressed on and the soldiers were weary, their throats parched. On the twelfth day, those in his advance guard brought Alexander a helmet containing a cup or two of water that they had been able to find. The troops watched with envy as the water was presented to him.

Alexander never hesitated. He dumped the water on the hot sand at his feet and said, "It's no use for one to drink when many thirst." His troops desperately needed water, but what he had in his helmet represented only a drop or two for each individual.
He didn't have the quantity of water they needed, but he gave them something else – inspiration. They found water later, but at that moment he gave them something that was more important – leadership.

huge difference between dumping information and truly communicating.)

Respectful partnering and participative leadership means that we don't act like cowards, making secret layoff decisions behind closed doors, hiding behind press releases, and getting external consultants or the HR department to do the dirty work of laying people off. Management can be tough, but leadership takes real courage. We can pay the price now or pay a much bigger price later.

How do you lead people to change? Start with that person in the mirror.

I'LL GO FIRST

A man should first direct himself in the way he should go. Only then should he instruct others.

BUDDHA

The CLEMMER Group did an extensive assessment with a divisional manager to diagnose the strengths and weaknesses within his division and implement a major change and improvement process. Our assessment report showed that the problems in the division's customer service, quality, and productivity could be traced to one cause – the management team was dysfunctional. They were technicians and managers, not leaders. Their individual and collective leadership was weak. After reviewing the report with the division manager, we planned an off-site retreat with the management team to review the report and establish action plans. On the first morning of the retreat, the division manager presented everyone with a beautiful folder printed with the company logo and the words "Change Kit: Change Begins Here" on the outside. Upon opening the folder, each manager found a large mirror inside.

Leadership isn't 'me-first'

"It was awful," she explained. "I was walking down Elm Street and there was a terrible accident. A man was thrown from his car and he was lying in the middle of the street. His leg was broken, his skull was fractured, and there was blood everywhere. Thank God I took that first-aid course."

"What did you do?" he asked.

"I sat down and put my head between my knees to keep from fainting!"

"Who are you going to believe, me or your own eyes?"
GROUCHO MARX

As a parent I am too often reminded of the old adage that says "children act like their parents – despite all attempts to teach them good manners." When one of our kids does something I'm not especially pleased with, my first inclination is to wonder "where did you learn that?" If I reflect on it for a while, I can start to see where that behavior came from – their mother, of course!

Well, maybe not. If I am really honest and take a long look in the leadership mirror, I can see there's no point in trying to put the blame elsewhere. But it is often tough to recognize our own behavior. It's even tougher to admit to it. In my leadership training and coaching work with managers, I often see a variation of the old parenting adage: team members act like their leader – despite all attempts to train them otherwise.

I can't build a team or organization different from me. I can't change them into something I am not. That was the main theme of my third book, *Pathways to Performance: A Guide to Transforming Yourself, Your Team, and Your Organization*. This theme came from working with so many managers who bought our training programs or hired our consultants to implement such things as customer-service programs, quality-improvement processes, and culture changes. Too often the characteristics or skill sets they were trying to build in their organizations weren't being modeled by the managers. This was like a single person – someone who's never even been able to get a second date – providing marriage counseling.

Too often we see managers with a poor service ethic who don't serve the servers trying to improve customer service. Managers with laughable personal time-management habits try to build process-discipline into their organization. Managers with little vision or boldness want more creative thinking. Managers who spend no time on the Internet and print off their emails try to implement e-business strategies. Managers with sloppy work habits try to improve quality. Managers who don't follow through and keep commitments want more accountability in their organizations. Managers who show up late for meetings (or cancel them at the last minute) want a more disciplined organization. Caustic managers sarcastically tell team members to provide more respectful customer service. Managers who make snide remarks about their peers or other groups want more teamwork. Managers blaming "them" and making excuses for their own performance want to improve morale. Management teams with slow decision-making processes want to build fast, flexible, and highly responsive organizations.

The message here, of course, is that changing them won't succeed unless it is preceded by changing me. As Mahatma Gandhi said, "We must be the change we wish to see in this world." It's all too easy to come up with changes I'd like to see in others. It takes a lot more leadership courage to change me in order to change them.

We've all heard about the importance of leading by example. Unfortunately, this phrase has become such a worn-out cliché that it has lost its meaning. Everywhere we look today, there are examples of our failure to recognize words and actions that don't match – like the sign on the door of a repair shop:

WE CAN REPAIR ANYTHING
(Please knock hard on the door… the bell doesn't work)

One manager hired me to speak to his organization about the work-life balance themes in *Growing the Distance*. This was an ongoing theme for their last few annual conferences. A participant told me later that last year's conference required everyone to travel on the Sunday to attend the Monday-morning kick-off. That Sunday was Father's Day.

Like a good ship's captain, leaders rely upon reports from their crew in order to navigate through treacherous waters.

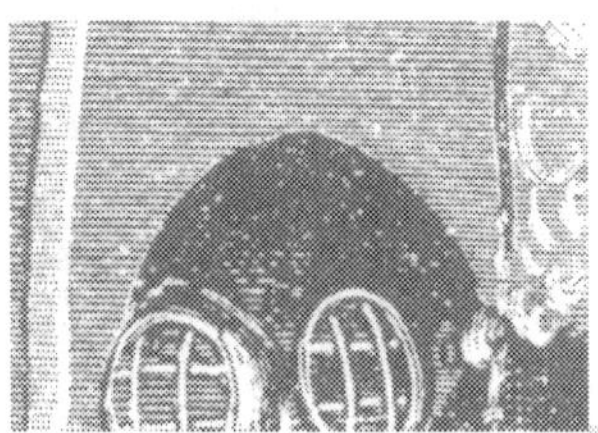

Perception and Reality

In a longitudinal study of the effectiveness of leaders... how subordinates assessed the leader proved most predictive of the leader's success and effectiveness, both at two and four years following the assessment. Even after seven years, the subordinates' assessments were predicting the leader's success – and with far more accuracy than the boss's own assessments. The subordinates' views were every bit as accurate a predictor as were much more elaborate ratings based on performance simulations done in assessment centers.

Daniel Goleman, Richard Boyatzis and Annie McKee, *Primal Leadership: Realizing the Power of Emotional Intelligence*

In 1707, Great Britain lost four warships and 2,000 sailors on the rocks of the Scilly Islands, located off the southwest coast of England. It wasn't that the location of the rocks was unknown; indeed, the maps of the area were clear and accurate. The problem was the ships' location. On that dark and foggy night, Admiral

Don't wait to see the blood

At our youngest daughter's sixth birthday party, a five-year-old boy hit Vanessa on the head. Asked to apologize, he politely refused: "Mr. Clemmer, I don't apologize unless I see teeth marks or blood."

Many managers don't realize the problems they're creating unless they see the teeth marks or blood on those with whom they work. The most insensitive managers are those who lack good feedback systems and refuse to seek input on how to improve their own performance.

Feedback is as critical to learning and improvement as cake is to a six-year-old's birthday party. As painful as I find "corrective feedback" and "suggestions for improvement," they are sources of my best learning and most profound personal changes.

Clowdisley Shovell and his navigators tragically miscalculated exactly where they were.

For thousands of years ships were smashed to bits on the rocks of well-charted hazards like shoals or islands. Often this happened on much-traveled routes where the hazards were well known to navigators. But knowing the position of rocks on a map isn't of much help when you don't know where on the map you are.

Whether on the high seas or in a corporate boardroom, maps, charts, or plans are very useful in plotting a course to where we want to go. But they are useless if we don't know where we are now. To get from here to there, we need to know where "here" is.

Rocks? What rocks?

With today's very precise GPS (Global Positioning Systems) and other technological aids, ships and planes are now able to see exactly where they are. As a result, these craft are able to avoid colliding with natural hazards, even in the most severe weather conditions.

There are numerous modern technologies, instruments, and techniques to help managers see where they are today. But many of them still attempt to navigate their own personal development or organization-change processes with tools similar to old-fashioned sextants or star charts. Some may have lookouts posted in the crow's nest, but ignore or discount any warnings that don't coincide with their own perception. With such crude and ineffective feedback systems, it's not surprising that managers often have no idea where they really are. Yet this often leads them to believe that things are going well. "Nobody's telling me about any problems," they say confidently as they steer their ship blindly toward the rocks.

Leaders, on the other hand, use more effective "instruments" to pinpoint exactly where they are and where they need to go next to reach their destination. They use informal and formal feedback channels, such as 360-degree feedback surveys. (These provide anonymous and blindly compiled input from all around me, including people I lead directly, my peers, my boss, as well as our internal/external customers.) Other tools include:

- Conducting project reviews
- Reversing performance appraisals with team members
- Hallway conversations
- Reflective time at meetings
- Grapevine chatter
- Appointing devil's advocates
- Chatting over a coffee or beer
- Focus groups
- Organization surveys
- Operational reviews
- Off-site retreats
- Input from consultants
- Organization/team assessments
- Mentors
- Networking
- External executive coaches

An old Yiddish saying teaches, "If one or two people tell you that you're an ass, you can ignore them. But if three or four people tell you you're an ass, you might think about putting on a saddle." Not knowing how those I am trying to lead perceive me is like sailing my ship without the feedback of navigational instruments.

Seeing through their eyes

Leaders know that it is hard to see the bigger picture when you're inside the frame. That's why they regularly step back to see themselves, their team, or their organization through the eyes of others. This means dealing with their perceptions as their reality. Effective leaders don't negate the viewpoint of others with comments like "that's just their perception, that's not reality." Leaders know that leadership, like beauty, is in the eye of the beholder. If people don't think I am providing leadership – even though I may think I am – they will act on that belief and respond accordingly.

If I want to change their perception and action, I need first to be fully aware of what their perception is. Then I can decide to change my behavior, try to change their perception, or both.

What do I see?

Poor managers are like vampires. You hold up a mirror and they see nothing.

Feedback-impaired managers are usually in favor of performance measurement and accountability – for everyone else.

We first noticed this connection when we were trying to understand why some teams or organizations had rich and powerful flows of performance data and rigorous measurements. But many other organizations that seemed equally determined to improve had very weak performance measurements. It didn't seem to be a knowledge issue. These low measurement organizations knew all about "360 degree" feedback systems, performance gap analysis, data-based tools and techniques, and the like.

But it was a lot of talk. There was little application. Then we noticed how people tip-toed around sensitive issues, especially problems that should have been raised with their immediate managers. We began to take note of the number of conversations we were having about how people tried to gauge a senior manager's mood to see if today was a good day to raise a sensitive issue or flag a problem. We also noticed how many managers claimed that they wanted to build a learning organization, then did little to learn how people in their organization perceived their behavior.

Personal feedback – especially about problems or faulty signals we've sent – can be very painful. But our frequency, sensitivity, and action (or lack of it) on personal performance feedback sets the learning and improvement pace and tone for the rest of our organization.

Sometimes a problem is obvious to everyone. So why don't we want to talk about it?

THE MOOSE ON THE TABLE

The day soldiers stop bringing you their problems is the day you have stopped leading them. They have either lost confidence that you can help them or concluded that you do not care. Either case is a failure of leadership.

COLIN POWELL, U.S. SECRETARY OF STATE

Imagine a team meeting around a conference-room table. They are reviewing operations and making plans. Charts are reviewed, slides are projected, documents are handed out, and calculations are made.

Now imagine that standing in the middle of the conference-room table is a great big moose.

Hearing the hard truths

"During World War II, Winston Churchill worried that his own larger-than-life personality would deter subordinates from bringing him bad news. So he set up a unit outside his generals' chain of command, the Statistical Office, whose primary job was to feed him the starkest, most unvarnished facts. In a similar vein, Richard Schroth and Larry Elliott, authors of the book *How Companies Lie*, suggest designated 'counterpointers,' whose function is to ask the rudest questions possible. Such mechanisms take information and turn it into information that can't be ignored... Even when a boss doesn't intend to quash dissent, subtle signals – a sour expression, a curt response – can broadcast the message that bad news isn't welcome."

"WHY COMPANIES FAIL," *FORTUNE*

No one says a word about the moose. Everyone carries on polite and earnest conversation as if this situation is very normal. Meanwhile the moose is eating papers at one end of the table while plopping out moose pies at the other end of the table splattering a few participants' business suits. Team members are passing papers around the moose's legs. They shift in their chairs to make eye contact with each other under the moose's belly or to see past it to the front of the room. Papers need to be pried out from underneath the moose's huge hoofs. When the moose lifts its head, his massive antlers poke into the meeting room ceiling, raining down chunks of ceiling tile and knocking out a light. No one says a thing about this. The leader carries on blissfully with the meeting.

As you've probably guessed by now, this is not a real scenario (at least, not in my experience!), but a symbolic one. The moose represents an issue that everyone knows is a problem but isn't being addressed. People are trying to carry on as if things are normal. Meanwhile the issue is blocking progress and has caused some team members to tune out of conversations. Like a dysfunctional family with an abuser in its midst, no one wants to confront the problem. By failing to declare the issue, they further empower it. The moose grows bigger.

The Moose-on-the-Table scenario is one that we run into very often with management teams. The problem is that conversations among the team aren't authentic. They don't deal with the real issues that are blocking progress. Some teams have a huge moose to deal with; others have a smaller moose.

Some teams have a whole moose family crowding them out. Do you have a moose on your table? Here are a few symptoms:

- The real conversations happen in the hallways or office after the meeting. There the moose or issues are clearly named.
- Team members complacently agree to a consensus at the meeting – then go off and do their own thing. They don't voice their disagreements for fear that they'll be labeled as not being team players.
- Commitments aren't kept and deadlines are missed. It's considered whining or copping out for a team member to give his or her real opinion about the feasibility of the target.
- Once the team manager gives his or her opinion, everyone else stays quiet or falls in line behind the manager. Team members suck up to the boss and pretend the moose doesn't exist.
- Sudden surprises often come "out of the blue" – especially from within the organization. The team manager is frequently surprised to see a simmering problem suddenly erupt into a full-blown crisis.
- The manager dominates meetings and most conversations. If he or she wants any of your ideas, he or she will give them to you.

ALL FIRED UP

When people care deeply about their work, they don't need to be pushed into performing at their best.

PASSION AND COMMITMENT

You can buy a man's time; you can buy his physical presence at a given place; you can even buy a measured number of his skilled muscular motions per hour. But you cannot buy enthusiasm... you cannot buy loyalty... you can not buy the devotion of hearts, minds, or souls. You must earn these.

CLARENCE FRANCIS, CHAIRMAN OF GENERAL FOODS DURING THE 1950S

The leadership vacuum found in many organizations often shows up in how managers try to buy passion and commitment. They push rather than pull. They manage rather than lead. This saps passion and reduces the "commitment culture" so vital to high performance. The Gallup organization found that only 29% of U.S. employees are engaged in their work. A Towers Perrin survey showed that 13% of employees surveyed were aggressively seeking new jobs and 45% were passive job-seekers who would consider other offers. More than 90% of people surveyed in a *Psychology Today* study aspired to producing the highest quality work possible. But less than 50% said they only work hard enough to keep their jobs. The main reason they gave for this big difference was frustration with management practices.

A reliable indicator of management's failure to impassion people and foster their commitment is absenteeism. When I was a kid I didn't enjoy school very much. So I was sick a lot. Once I found my life work and pursued career choices that really turned me on, my health improved miraculously. In more than 30 years, I have taken fewer than five sick days.

Unexciting organizations are paying a huge price for their managers' failure to engage the hearts of people. When I am excited about my work – when I feel like a valued partner and have a commitment to my team and to reaching our goals together – I am much less likely to call in sick. When I feel like my boss doesn't care much about me, if my work is boring and routine, if I am just a pair of hired hands, the group I am part of is not really a team, I don't know and don't really care what our organization does or what customers think about our products and services, then I will call in sick at the first sniffle. Not to mention that feeling down lowers my immune system and makes me much more susceptible to what ever bugs are going around.

Enriching jobs for fun and profit

Making jobs more rewarding is the best way to influence motivation and job satisfaction. It involves introducing variety into the workplace in terms of skill and responsibilities, emphasizing the importance and significance of the job employees have, providing a degree of autonomy, and sharing regular feedback. It also requires giving employees more control over the processes they are involved in for real empowerment.

Job enrichment might be used in accounting by giving a clerk the responsibility to interact with other departments, make changes to a process, or approve certain requests without having to ask for management review. Enrichment could be used in manufacturing by training people in several job functions, so they acquire different skills and are able to contribute in different ways. Enrichment could be participation on a processes improvement team. It could involve soliciting and using worker input, or improving processes or systems that support employees in their jobs, such as a requisition process or computer system.

William Denney, author and consultant, Malcolm Baldrige National Quality Award examiner, Certified Quality Manager and Auditor

Leaders inspire people from within. They ignite the internal passion that fires self-motivation.

Emotional Empowerment

Our passion for productivity increasingly depends upon the productivity of our passions. We can't divorce commitment and caring from efficiency and effectiveness.

Michael Schrage, Co-director of MIT Media Labs' e-market initiative and author of *Serious Play*

What gets people really excited about their jobs? What inspires the passion and commitment that translates into exceptional performance? It isn't a process of management controls. It's a leadership function that instills in people an emotional stake in what they do. As Daniel Goleman and his co-authors report in *Primal Leadership: Realizing the Power of Emotional Intelligence*, "Great leaders move us. They ignite our passion and inspire the best in us. When we try to explain why they are so effective, we speak of strategy, vision, or powerful ideas. But the reality is much more primal: Great leadership works through the emotions."

Where such leadership is lacking, we see correspondingly low levels of passion and commitment. This manifests itself in many ways. Some of the symptoms include "we-they" gaps between organizational levels (such as frontline staff and management) or between groups and departments, poor levels of customer service, lower quality, dwindling morale, Victimitis, low pride, and little ownership.

People who hate their work are slaves, no matter how much money they make. Managers who "motivate" by pushing – rather than pulling to lead – can too easily become slave drivers. They can become like a misguided farmer who angrily kicks his cow in the stomach because her milk production is off.

Internal vs. external motivators

Most managers recognize that one of their key roles is "motivating" others. They also recognize that a key to motivation is empowerment. But it's too often a lot of empty "leaderspeak." For all that the popular "E" word has been bandied about in the last few years, not much has changed in many organizations.

There are many reasons why empty empowerment rhetoric is so widespread today. One of the most common is confusion about (or misapplication of) intrinsic or internal motivation (leadership) versus extrinsic or external motivators (management). In his article "Empowerment: The Emperor's New Clothes," Harvard professor Chris Argyris outlines this difference:

"If management wants employees to take more responsibility for their own destiny, it must encourage the development of internal commitment. As the name implies, internal commitment comes largely from within. . . .by definition, internal commitment is participatory and very closely allied with empowerment. The more that management wants internal commitment from its employees, the more it must try to involve employees in defining work objectives, specifying how to achieve them, and setting stretch targets."

The power of using employee involvement to build internal commitment is both measurable and impressive. One organization made a massive effort to involve everyone in their planning process. (In our consulting work, there's an old adage that we frequently quote to clients: "If they help plan the battle, they won't battle the plan.") A year later the company's absenteeism dropped by 300% – and saved millions of dollars!

Satisfied frontline servers create satisfied customers.

COMMITMENT CONNECTIONS

We found that there was a cause-and-effect relationship between the two; that it was impossible to maintain a loyal customer base without a base of loyal employees; and that the best employees prefer to work for companies that deliver the kind of superior value that builds customer loyalty... building loyalty has in fact become the acid test of leadership.

FREDERICK REICHHELD, *THE LOYALTY EFFECT* AND *LOYALTY RULES*

For most organizations, the goal of improving customer service levels is an article of faith. And so it should be, because there's an overwhelming body of research to show that building customer loyalty has a major impact on profitability. In fact, according to one study – based on 46,000 business-to-business surveys – a "totally satisfied" customer contributes 2.6 times as much revenue as a "somewhat satisfied" customer.

The University of Michigan Business School's National Quality Research Center has conducted one of the most extensive ongoing studies on customer satisfaction. Since 1994, the Center has tracked the American Customer Satisfaction Index (ACSI). "Year after year and quarter after quarter, the ACSI demonstrates a definite link between customer satisfaction and financial metrics such as market value added, stock price, and return on investment," concludes director Claes Fornell. "Satisfied customers reward companies with repeat business which has a huge effect on profits."

Keeping the promise of customer service

A company's external customer service is only as strong as the company's internal leadership, and the culture of commitment that this leadership creates. To paraphrase Abraham Lincoln, our service or brand promise can't fool all of our customers all of the time. If the service messages are out of step with what's ultimately experienced by customers, marketing dollars are wasted. And customer dissatisfaction rises right along with staff turnover. Scott Cook, founder of Intuit (creators of Quicken software), puts it this way; "Great brands are earned, not bought. Customer experience is where brand is built, not in the marketing budget."

Clearly, there are significant benefits to be realized from trying to improve an organization's service/quality. And that's why managers devote so much time and money to training programs that "instruct" employees on the specifics of dealing with customers. What these managers don't understand, however, is that such attempts are largely cosmetic. Real improvements in customer service start with providing superior service and support to the employees themselves.

All too often, this misunderstanding results in sending staff through "smile training," issuing edicts to be more courteous, or teaching them how to handle dissatisfied customers. In the meantime, processes and systems don't support frontline servers. Irritants and issues that reduce morale are swept aside as excuses. An airline manager attempted to address the problem of declining customer satisfaction by issuing a directive urging staff to smile and be nicer to passengers. A flight attendant's response showed how that manager just didn't get it: "We're smiling in spite of the fact that we're doing our job one, two or three flight attendants short, with equipment that often doesn't work properly and with a product that has deteriorated."

Harvard professor and author Rosabeth Moss Kanter likens this type of change-effort to putting lipstick on a bulldog. Rather than deal with an ugly and nasty problem (my apologies to bulldog owners), the manager makes superficial changes and tries to pass them off as real improvements. The result of this cosmetic effort is, as Kanter observes, that "the bulldog's appearance hasn't improved, but now it's really angry."

Going the extra mile

Taking an organization from good to great customer service ultimately depends on the people who provide that service. It can only happen through the volunteerism – the willingness to go beyond what is merely required – of people who serve on the front lines. Going from ordinary to extraordinary performance happens through the discretionary efforts of frontline staff deciding to make the thousands of "moment of truth" (any time a customer interacts with the company in person, by phone, or electronically), they manage every day as positively as they possibly can. This enthusiasm, loyalty, or devotion can't be forced on people. It only happens through a "culture of commitment," where frontline people reflect to the outside the intense pride and ownership they are experiencing on the inside.

Satisfaction at work

"The best predictor of customer satisfaction among workplace attributes is what Vanderbilt professor Roland Rust calls service climate: those attributes of overall workplace climate that characterize how well equipped employees are to deliver customer service, such as the adequacy of resources and equipment and job skills development."

For every one percent increase in internal service climate there is a two percent increase in revenue.

In cardiac care units where nurses' moods were depressed, patient death rates were four times higher than in comparable units.

Cornell's School of Hotel Administration found that employees' emotional commitment and sense of identity with the company is a key factor in providing excellent service.

A study of call centers found that "satisfied contact center employees make for satisfied and loyal customers... customers decide whether or not to make future purchasing decisions with a company, or to recommend its services to others, as a direct result of their experiences with a contact center representative... key indicators of contact center representative satisfaction include relationships with co-workers and management, job challenges, and frequency of development or training opportunities... sense of pride with their job and within the overall company.

Involvement and participation can turn disinterested people into committed stakeholders.

PERFORMANCE PARTNERS

"Organizations should be built and managers should be functioning so people can be naturally empowered. If someone's doing their job... they should know their job better than anybody. They don't need to be 'empowered,' but encouraged and left alone to be able to do what they know best."

HENRY MINTZBERG, MANAGEMENT RESEARCHER AND AUTHOR

A tale of two managers

Joel views himself as a "realist." As a manager, he has little time or patience for, as he puts it, "making nicey-nicey." Coming from a deep technical background, he hates meetings ("they get in the way of real work") and resents having to sell changes or get people on board. "I don't care if they like me," he's fond of saying, "I only want their respect and compliance." He likes nothing better than solving tough technical problems with practical, well-designed solutions. He runs his organization "by the numbers." He focuses on continuously improving existing processes and technologies. He sets high targets and relentlessly drives everyone to meet them.

The part of the job Joel likes least is dealing with people. Their irrational, emotional behavior drives him nuts.

He often dismisses contrary points of view with comments like, "that's only their perception, that's not reality." He then proceeds to prove his point with facts, rational arguments, and analysis.

Joel believes that most people see their work as a four-letter word and must therefore be tightly controlled, threatened, or bribed with incentives before they will work hard enough. He prides himself on being a tough manager who rolls up his sleeves and digs deep into operational details. He exercises tight control with policies, directives, and rules. His mood-swings cause the team's emotional tone to wildly gyrate from high to low with much time being spent figuring out how to read him and avoid his wrath. Joel's main tool for influencing behavior on his team is through punishment and "shooting down people who haven't done their homework."

Denise is an "idealist" with a strong technical background. She realized some time ago that her real leadership work increasingly gets done in meetings. So she has trained and worked hard at developing her facilitation and team leadership skills. She also knows that just wishing or "positive thinking" problems away usually makes them worse. She is also determined not to be so focused on the problem that she and her team can't see the possibilities. To avoid getting stuck in "reality ruts," Denise keeps everyone focused on what could be.

Denise sees possibilities in people. She believes that people want to take pride in their work and be part of a winning team. She has learned that motivation or morale problems are usually rooted in leaders failing to engage people in the broader aims and ideals of the organization. As more people search for meaning in their lives and in their work, this disconnect creates much of the frustration and lack of purpose found in so many workplaces today. Denise works hard at connecting people to her organization's vision, values, and purpose. Denise's high energy and optimistic attitude sets a strong and positive emotional tone throughout her organization. People are inspired to face tough problems with confidence and teamwork.

Out in the real world, we see plenty of Joels – and not nearly enough Denises. Their differences are obvious enough, but ask yourself the following questions:

- Whom would you rather work for?
- Who is the stronger leader?
- Who is likely to get the best results?
- Would your team consider you to be most like Joel or Denise? How do you *know*?

Denise uses a collaborative approach to partner with people. She sees people as adults who are generally self-managing (with some exceptions). Joel treats them like kids who need to be managed "with a firm hand" (with some exceptions). Denise cares about people. Joel dehumanizes and objectifies them. Denise uses the power of persuasion (leadership) to get things done. Joel uses position power (management). Denise builds a cause and case for change, appealing to the head and heart to get buy-in. Joel tries to overcome resistance to change with facts and force; like someone traveling in a foreign country who can't speak the local language, he'll just talk louder to be understood. Denise shares as much information as she can and builds strong multi-channel and multi-directional communication loops. Joel gives people information on a need-to-know basis; he only "empowers" people as a motivational technique to get people to do what he wants done. Denise partners with people so they feel naturally empowered to reach their mutual goals.

Building passion and commitment the Wal-Mart way

In response to the much-asked question "What is Wal-Mart's secret to success?" founder Sam Walton compiled a list of his business principles. Here are some of those which pertain especially to providing the leadership that creates passion and commitment:

Commit to your business. Believe in it more than anybody else. I think I overcame every single one of my personal shortcomings by the sheer passion I brought to my work. If you love your work, you'll be out there every day trying to do it the best you possibly can, and pretty soon everybody around will catch the passion from you – like a fever.

Share your profits with all your Associates, and treat them as partners. In turn, they will treat you as a partner, and together you will all perform beyond your wildest expectations... behave as a servant leader in a partnership.

Communicate everything you possibly can to your partners. The more they know, the more they'll understand. The more they understand, the more they'll care. Once they care, there's no stopping them. If you don't trust your Associates to know what's going on, they'll know you don't really consider them partners. Information is power, and the gain you get from empowering your Associates more than offsets the risk of informing your competitors.

Appreciate everything your Associates do for the business. A paycheck and a stock option will buy one kind of loyalty. But all of us like to be told how much somebody appreciates what we do for them. We like to hear it often, and especially when we have done something we're really proud of. Nothing else can quite substitute for a few well-chosen, well-timed, sincere words of praise. They're absolutely free – and worth a fortune.

Celebrate your successes. Find some humor in your failures. Don't take yourself so seriously. Loosen up, and everybody around you will loosen up. Have fun. Show enthusiasm – always. When all else fails, put on a costume and sing a silly song. Then make everybody else sing with you. Don't do a hula on Wall Street. It's been done. Think up your own stunt. All of this is more important, and more fun, than you think, and it really fools the competition. "Why should we take those cornballs at Wal-Mart seriously?"

Listen to everyone in your company. And figure out ways to get them talking. The folks on the front lines – the ones who actually talk to the customer – are the only ones who really know what's going on out there. You'd better find out what they know. This really is what total quality is all about. To push responsibility down in your organization, and to force good ideas to bubble up within it, you must listen to what your Associates are trying to tell you.

The evidence clearly shows that building partnerships through involvement and participation (like Denise's approach) is the strong leadership that leads to high performance:

- A study by J. Howard & Associates in a large insurance company found that the 20% of managers that were seen as least inclusive ran the least profitable units. This contrasts with the 20% of managers considered to be the most inclusive who had units with 60% higher profitability. They also had lower turnover rates and higher customer satisfaction ratings.

- In an article entitled "Happy Companies Make Happy Investments," *Fortune* reports that "you can make a killing by making nice." Companies on the annual 100 Best Companies to Work For lists had an average return on investment of 18.2%, versus the S&P 500 average of 5.7% during that same time period. "So managers, be kind and honest. Your employees and shareholders will thank you."

- "Companies that adopt employee involvement measures such as work teams and employee participation in decision making, are likely to find significant rewards on their bottom line," says a report produced by the University of Southern California's Marshall School of Business. They found that the average return on sales was 8.3% among low-involvement companies versus 10.4% among high-involvement firms. Stock price appreciation was 21% versus 44%.

- A study of franchise systems found that one of the greatest differentiators among the most successful franchisees was "a belief that employees deserve trust, enjoy responsibility and offer meaningful contributions to the business." One of the study's researchers concluded, "The managers who involve their employees were much more successful in the performance of their franchise than those who distrust employees and exclude them from decisions."

- A study by Success Profiles analyzed the relationship between effectively giving people authority to make decisions and compounded revenue growth. They found that companies who scored "Poor" in this key leadership practice had a 2.3% compound growth rate. Those companies that scored "Very Good" on giving authority to make decisions had an 11.1% rate of compound growth!

Partnering promotes health and safety

Judith Erickson runs a consulting practice specializing in decreasing injuries and accidents in the workplace by evaluating the organizational factors impacting safely performance. Some of her findings:

"Companies with the lowest lost-time injury rates were those with the highest level of management commitment and employee involvement...

...the management characteristic most predictive of high safety performance is a positive employee environment... [which] included caring for and respecting employees, open communication, and employee involvement and participation....

...there is a definite relationship among safety performance, productivity, quality, worker job satisfaction, and reduced occupational stress and employee sabotage...

...when management encourages employees to participate in decision-making, safety performance is higher... employees are treated as a valuable resource rather than as a cost of doing business; they are treated as individuals and with respect...

...when management expresses an ethical concern for employees, safety performance is higher...when employees are aware of management's genuine interest in them, they will respond in kind. In this type of an environment, employee innovative thinking, suggestions and decision-making evolve, to the benefit of the employee and the organization alike. One tangible benefit is fewer injuries."

Partners talk to each other

"The man who gets the most satisfactory results is not always the man with the most brilliant single mind, but rather the man who can best coordinate the brains and talents of his associates."

Sir William Alton Jones, 18th-century English philologist and jurist

When faced with major organizational problems, managers often hire consultants to help provide a solution. The consultant will usually interview people, run focus groups, and gather input from a variety of sources. Many good ideas are sifted through and the most relevant one presented to management along with the consultant's recommended action plan.

As a company that does a lot of this kind of work, we don't find the practice objectionable! What saddens us is how frequently the ideas that most excite managers are ones that have existed inside the organization for years. Yet managers are often hearing them for the first time. Or they are finally paying attention because the ideas are coming from outside experts. This points to a major failure of leadership within the organization.

In such cases, managers often will have tried to solicit ideas using various formalized approaches, such as suggestion boxes. These are rarely effective. A disgruntled staff member once put a sign on a suggestion box that summed up the consensus view of this approach: "Please don't put any more ideas in here. The handle is broken and it won't flush." Instead, the organization needs to focus on the leadership values of partnership, participation, and involvement. Without these values, there is no system that can foster the communication necessary to keep ideas flowing.

Success Profiles studied 150 companies to understand the impact of "a business excelling in Feedback and Engagement where employees work each day in an environment where their feedback is elicited, valued, and acted upon." They found the companies that best met this description experienced revenue growth many times higher than those companies with low levels of feedback and engagement. They also studied organizational communication and employee access to information, and discovered that "companies demonstrating poor performance in this business practice had nearly twice the employee turnover as those companies achieving only average performance."

Low commitment has a high cost.

Retaining Top People

A leader will only command the level of loyalty he or she is willing to give to others.

Winston Churchill

Attracting and retaining talented people is a growing challenge for many organizations. Demographic projections show that this issue will become ever more critical as the large group of people in the "baby boom" begins to retire. Competition for the best people will intensify. The most successful organizations will be those "magnet companies" that attract and hang on to good people. Their management reputation or "leadership brand" will become as critical to their success as the company brand they are selling in their marketplace. Internal-cultural and external-marketing brands will become ever more intertwined.

Many managers badly underestimate the high costs of turnover. Some examples:

- A trucking company found that it could increase profits by 50% by cutting driver turnover in half.
- One study estimated it costs a typical information technology company $34,100 for each lost programmer,

$10,455 to replace a specialty store retail clerk, and $6,926 for a call center representative.

Other estimates of the cost of turnover range from 25% of salary to as much as a full year's pay. (This wide variation can be attributed to the difficulty of estimating the impact of customer dissatisfaction and retention and the lowered efficiencies for everyone who works with, trains, and supports the new replacement.) In high-turnover organizations, the problem is complicated and compounded by a vicious circle: On the one hand, they don't invest heavily in people because they might leave and take all that expensive training with them; on the other, if they don't invest in people, the chances increase that they won't stick around when a better offer comes along.

Creating commitment cultures

After 20 years of research and 60,000 exit interviews, the Saratoga Institute reports that 80% of turnover is related to unsatisfactory relationships with the boss. Talent retention and engagement will remain one of management's highest priorities over the coming years. Indeed, in the so-called new economy with its ever-increasing reliance on talent and technology, retention and engagement are critical to an organization's survival.

Organizations therefore need to focus on three areas to retain and engage their talented people:

Employee development – Support learning and growth.

Find ways to continuously develop and grow workers' talents.

Enrich and enliven employees' work, making every effort to increase the time they spend on desirable and innovative work.

Help workers identify opportunities for moving laterally and vertically.

Link workers to mentors, coaches, leaders, or colleagues who can offer guidance and support.

Management style – Inspire loyalty.

Ask employees what they want from their work and what it takes to keep them.

Provide constant feedback – clearly, truthfully, and respectfully – and, in return, listen closely and carefully.

Look for creative, meaningful ways to recognize and reward workers.

Create a culture of inclusion – valuing not only differences of race and gender, but thoughts, experiences, and attitudes as well.

Hold managers accountable for retention and then give them the training and the tools to do it.

Work environment – Create one that people love.

Let fun happen.

Share information freely and regularly.

Give people space – providing the freedom to get the job done in ways that work best for them, from their schedule and attire to their approach and process."

Beverly Kaye and Sharon Jordan-Evans, *Love 'Em or Lose 'Em: Getting Good People to Stay*

Strong leaders are 'people magnets'

There are many complex reasons why some organizations are more successful than others in attracting and retaining the best people. However, studies reveal some common patterns. The most significant of these clearly boil down to questions of leadership.

- A study of 200 high-potential leaders from 120 worldwide companies found that providing a challenge and excitement about the work and the mission of the organization, giving recognition, and helping people follow their dreams had the greatest impact on retention rates.

- A WorkLife Design survey reviewed the characteristics that made organizations employers of choice. Only 34% named pay. About 56% said flexible benefits were a major factor. A whopping 80% of respondents said the work environment was the biggest factor. This was described as servant leadership, trust and cooperation, family friendly policies, work-life balance, and credible and fair management.

- Ipsos-Reid asked employees what makes them stay in a job and what makes them consider another offer. Employees reported, in order of importance, that they will stay in their current jobs if: they like the work (78 percent); they like their co-workers (68 percent); they like the mission and activities of the company (61 percent); they are learning a lot (57 percent); they are satisfied with salary (53 percent).

Curt Coffman, co-author of *First, Break all the Rules: What the World's Greatest Managers Do Differently* and *Follow this Path: How the World's Greatest Organizations Drive Growth by Unleashing Human Potential*, reflects on key findings from the

Gallup organization's massive study of leadership practices in hundreds of companies: "So, how do we build loyalty among our most productive and talented people? It begins and ends with the manager. Gallup research shows that people join companies, but they leave managers and supervisors." He explains that great "world-class" companies create work environments that are "more profitable (44% higher), more productive (50% higher), and have higher degrees of customer loyalty (50% higher)." Based on a study of over 1 million employees in 330 organizations worldwide, Ernest & Young concluded that "ineffective managers are a major factor in the increasing departure rates… poor managers have a huge impact on employee turnover."

Leaders foster individual passion and commitment.

The Power of One

Without passion man is a mere latent force and possibility, like the flint which awaits the shock of the iron before it can fire forth its spark.

Henry Amiel

Strong leaders are very good at aligning individual interests, strengths, and goals with the work that needs to be done. To paraphrase Joseph Campbell's famous dictum, they help people follow their bliss. Peter Drucker once observed, "Whenever anything is being accomplished, it is being done, I have learned, by a monomaniac with a mission."

Strong leaders harness the passion of the monomaniacs on their team to bring about change. Even if this passion is *against* the leader's change, it is still valuable since a leader knows that resistance to change is far better than apathy. The stronger the resistance, the stronger the energy that's available. So leaders dig deeper to understand the source of the resistance and either rethink the change based on the wisdom they uncover, or they harness and realign the energy of that resistance.

When a team member approaches the leader with an improvement suggestion (and this happens to leaders more frequently than to conventional managers), the leader will first probe to see how deep his or her passion might be for the change. If it's reasonably strong and the idea merits testing, the leader will often give the team member responsibility for trying out or implementing the change. This creates higher ownership and nurtures a team of people who get directly and actively involved in making improvements. This high-involvement leadership sharply contrasts with the traditional approach of frontline people making suggestions for management or other departments to implement – and then grumbling in the hallways that nobody ever acts on their suggestions.

Strong leaders engage people's hearts. They build ever-deeper passion and commitment. The key leadership word is "care." When we care about our work, we will often be harder on ourselves then anyone else would dare to be. When we really care about the customers we serve, we'll go out of our way to ensure that each "moment of truth" (contact with customers) is as positive as we can make it. When we care about making our organization successful, we'll go above and beyond our job to do whatever it takes to be part of a winning team. When we care about our products or services, we'll do what ever it takes to continue feeling proud of what we do.

Leaders care deeply about the people in their organization. Team members feel their care and reciprocate it.

Passionate for the right job

"Of all the decisions a manager makes, none is as important as the decisions about people because they determine the performance capacity of the organization... the goal is to make productive the specific strengths and knowledge of each individual."

PETER DRUCKER

An old bit of Texas wisdom teaches us that "you can put your boots in the oven, but that don't make them biscuits." Leaders know that nothing kills passion and commitment in their organization more than bad hiring and promotion decisions. That's why leaders spend a huge amount of time assessing new people they are hiring and everyone they're considering promoting.

The average manager will interview someone once or twice before making a hiring decision. Strong leaders will put candidates through four to six personal, peer, and team interviews. A study by the Center for Creative Leadership found that when one individual made hiring decisions for management positions, the newly hired manager was judged to be successful just 35% of the time. When a hiring team of four or five made the decision, success rose to 55%. But when the small group included both customers and subordinates, success rates soared to 70%.

Leaders don't try teaching frogs to fly

Once upon a time, a manager had a frog named Fred working on his team. One day, after returning from a strategic planning retreat, he called Fred into his office and enthusiastically proclaimed, "We're going to open up an air courier division! I'm going to teach you to fly!"

Fred responded, "I can't fly. I'm a frog, not a bird."

Disappointed at Fred's lack of passion and commitment, the manager told Fred, "That negative attitude of yours could be a real problem. I am putting you through a motivational program." So Fred attended motivational rallies and workshops, viewed inspiring videos, and read personal growth books.

On the first day of flying lessons, the manager could barely control his excitement. Fred could barely control his bladder. The manager explained that their office building had seven floors, and each day Fred would jump out of a window, starting at the first floor and eventually getting to the top floor. By the time they reached the top floor, Fred would surely be able to fly.

Fred pleaded for his life, but it fell on deaf ears. "He just isn't committed to this process," thought the manager. "But I won't let nay-sayers get in my way." With that, the manager opened the window and threw Fred off the first floor. Fred landed with a dull thud and almost killed an unemployed carrier pigeon hunting for crumbs on the sidewalk below.

The next day Fred begged not to be thrown out the window. The manager referred to a book on change management and read the part about how managers must always expect resistance when implementing new programs. Out the window went Fred with a splat.

This training routine continued through days three and four. Fred made ever bigger splats as he was tossed from the third and fourth floors. Now this was not to say that Fred wasn't trying his best. On the fifth day, after the manager urged him to fall smarter not harder, Fred flapped his legs madly in a vain attempt to fly. On the sixth day, he tied a small red cape around his neck and tried to think Superman thoughts.

By the seventh day, Fred accepted his fate and no longer begged for mercy. He simply looked at the manager and said, "You know you're killing me, don't you?" The manager pointed out that Fred failed to meet any of their performance goals. Fred said quietly, "Shut up and open the window." He leaped out, taking careful aim at the large jagged rock by the corner of the building. Fred went to that great lily pad in the sky.

MATTERS OF THE HEART

Leaders help us to find purpose in our work – and in our lives.

SPIRIT AND MEANING

The search for meaning is intrinsic to human nature. As thinking creatures, we want to understand why we find ourselves on this road and where the journey is taking us...we are wanderers, searching and striving for end and aim, for purpose and connection.

WILLIAM J. BENNETT, *THE MORAL COMPASS: STORIES FOR A LIFE'S JOURNEY*

When our daughter Vanessa was a young teenager, we hired her to do some after-school general administrative support work at The CLEMMER Group offices. She was delighted to earn an hourly wage for a variety of tasks. One of her jobs was to key-in selected passages from articles and book summaries for entry in my electronic research database. One evening she came home very frustrated. I asked her what the problem was. "Today I spent three hours keying-in text and then found out that it had already been done." Knowing that this had been the result of some miscommunication (from me, actually), I tried to console her: "You will still be paid for all your work." "Yeah," she admitted sourly, "but I hate doing useless work."

We all hate doing useless work. We are impassioned by meaningful work. We all want to make a buck; but it's not the same as making a difference. Of course, making a difference or doing something "meaningful" is very subjective and personal. What you and I find meaningful can be vastly different. Strong leaders know that a key to fostering individual passion and commitment is finding the "nobility" in every job. No matter how menial the task, leaders help frontline people feel proud of their work.

I once had a speaking engagement with a cleaning and custodial company at their annual management conference. Arriving early and sitting in on the meeting to get a feel for the group and the conference, I was inspired by what a remarkable job those leaders did of bringing "pride of craft" to clean toilets and shiny floors. They showed pictures of facilities before (good thing it wasn't near meal time) and after, gave awards and recognition, and discussed best cleaning practices – all with much more energy and professionalism than I had seen from many other highly trained and multi-degreed "professionals" at their meetings.

Let's be Frank (I): Getting all fired up

Frank is a manager for a technology company. (Some of you will know him from my previous book, *Growing the Distance.*) During the past year he's been through a major personal transformation. The hugely successful career everyone envied him for on the outside was merely a facade for the equally overwhelming unhappiness he felt on the inside. He was living in ever-increasing material prosperity while his spiritual poverty steadily worsened. Faced with work that was becoming ever more meaningless, and with his marriage to Debbie on the rocks, Frank, at his very lowest point, considered ending his life.

Frank recognized that something had to be done. With typical intensity, he began a personal quest to find deeper meaning in his life. After months of study, meditation, and clarifying his vision, values, and purpose, Frank broke through his "trapped emptiness." He developed a renewed sense of purpose. Life was worth living. He and Debbie began revitalizing their marriage and family life. He was now looking for ways to help his team connect with the same sense of meaning that Frank had been feeling.

Listening to the car radio on his way to work one morning, Frank heard a caller ask the host to play a special love song for his wife. The caller went on for some time about what a wonderful woman she was to have put up with 21 years of traveling more than 300 days per year while raising their three kids. Intrigued, the radio host asked the caller what he did for a living. "I'm in the circus," he answered. "And what do you do there?" she inquired. "I am the human cannonball," he replied.

Now the host was really fascinated. "Why in the world anyone would want to be shot out of a cannon several times a day?" she asked incredulously. Mr. Cannonball's response was immediate and enthusiastic: "Are you kidding me? This is the greatest job ever! People take time out of their busy lives to come spend a couple of hours with us under the Big Top. If we do a really good job we can take them away from all of their worries and stress and put a smile on their faces. They watch me come flying out of that cannon with my arms and legs flailing all over the place and land safely in the net. When I look up and see them laughing and in good spirits, I know I've done a wonderful thing for these folks. Maybe a couple of weeks later when they're having a bad day and life has got the best of them they'll think back to me flying out of that cannon with my arms and legs thrashing through the air. Just maybe it will get them smiling again and their day won't seem so bad after all. So you see," he concluded, "this really is a great job! It's a job I love and one I wouldn't trade for anything."

"Wow!" Frank exclaimed to himself. "Here's a guy with a job most of us would never dream of, but is able to find such deep spirit and meaning in his work. Why can't I help my team members do the same? There really is no job that can't be made fulfilling in some way. The big question is how."

High-performance organizations are often defined by people who feel connected to something greater than themselves.

'Meaning-Full' Work

It's like we have learned to build the world's best, most efficient fireplace. We have taken thermal science to an all-time high. The firebox is lined with eternal space age poly-something. A masterpiece of efficiency and design science. The only problem is that there is no fire. We have no fire in the fireplace. What, then, is the point of the fireplace?

Ian Percy, *Going Deep: Exploring Spirituality in Life and Leadership*

The timeless leadership principle of Spirit and Meaning creates a big disconnect for many managers. On the one hand, most managers are well aware that the emotional tone or spirit of a team or organization is vital to its success. The will to win, to excel, or to make a difference, is often what defines high performance in just about any human endeavor. It's one of those mighty forces that can't easily be counted, but creates the results that count.

On the other hand, spirit is also soft and nebulous. It's very hard to define. So figuring out how to increase it is a huge leadership challenge. There are no formulas or 12 easy steps to sure-fire success. Spirit doesn't fit neatly into traditional management activities such as planning, organizing, controlling, and coordinating. It is at odds with an unemotional business-is-business approach. Many managers have never been part of a highly spirited organization or deeply meaningful work team. They have never been led by a spirited leader who set an exciting emotional tone that resonated deeply with people throughout their organization.

An even greater challenge for many managers is that they haven't probed too deeply into their own sense of personal spirit and meaning. Many are not living purposeful lives of meaning, where their work is a rich source of connection to their own spirit. The hub of their own leadership wheel – personal vision, values, and purpose – isn't very strong. Not surprisingly, they have a tough time leading others to a place they've never really been themselves. We can't give what we don't have. It's very hard for a manager to bring spirit and meaning to a team when the hub of their leadership wheel is wobbling.

Spirituality in the workplace

"When I hear managers say they're going to be tough on their employees, I say to myself, 'Show me how you're going to get the commitment and enthusiasm you need from an educated work force with a fear-based approach.'"

IAN MITROFF, PROFESSOR, MARSHALL SCHOOL OF BUSINESS, UNIVERSITY OF SOUTHERN CALIFORNIA

Ian Mitroff and organizational consultant Elizabeth Denton extensively interviewed and surveyed managers to assess if it's appropriate to integrate spirituality into the management of an organization and whether spirituality can help make a company more profitable. Participants saw a big difference between religion and spirituality. They saw religion as very inappropriate for discussion in today's increasingly diverse workplaces. However, they felt that spirituality was very appropriate and highly desirable to talk about and express in the workplace.

The study showed that many people see spirituality giving a deeper and more fundamental grounding to values. A word that captures the essence of spirit in the workplace is "interconnectedness." Organizations and teams with strong spirit and deep meaning are highly interconnected and interdependent. Reflecting on his findings, Mitroff reports:

- "Those organizations that had a spiritual bent were perceived to significantly outperform those organizations that were utilitarian, i.e., bottom-line oriented."
- "All the evidence indicates that if you're going to manage spiritually it's going to be harder to do that than if you run a traditional organization... [however] you get a more committed work force – you get more of the total person coming to work."
- "The biggest risk is that people will think that they're really smuggling in religion in the guise of spirituality. Everybody is wary of that and the antennae are up."
- "This issue of 'the whole person at work' is important because we're hiring a more educated workforce. They want to develop to their full potential. They want to work for ethical organizations and to do interesting work."

A growing number of studies are now looking at the critical leadership issue of bringing spirit and meaning to organizations. One poll found that managers want a deeper sense of meaning and fulfillment on the job more than they want money and time off. Management consultants McKinsey & Co. found that "when companies engage in programs using spiritual techniques, productivity improves and turnover is greatly reduced." Former Harvard professor David Maister's study of the values most impacting organization effectiveness found that "'People treat each other with respect around here' turned out to be one of the nine profit predictors."

Ian Percy, author and keynote speaker on spirit and leadership, counterbalances discussions of The Learning Organization with fulfilling the need for "the yearning organization." In his book *Going Deep: Exploring Spirituality in Life and Leadership*, he writes, "There is an awakening happening all over the corporate world. In every culture. In every profession and corporate context. People are yearning for meaning....the sooner organizations realize that their real problems are spiritual problems, the sooner they will experience true transformation and not have to muck around in what are largely destructive strategies of re-engineering, right-sizing, rationalizing and so on."

Let's be Frank (II): In search of the company's lost heart

In the midst of that morning's operations review meeting, Frank starting wondering just how the company had lost its heart. As he looked around the room he saw nothing but stern faces, apprehensive expressions, and a few stifled yawns. The humorous quips he had added to the conversation a few minutes ago to lighten things up fell as flat as a day-old glass of Coke. Everyone was so serious. They solemnly reviewed yet more numbers and looked at more charts and graphs. Frank knew that management issues were critical to success. Facts, processes, systems, data – all were vital to efficient operations. But how did the company become so unbalanced? When did efficiency crowd out effectiveness? How had the management vampire been able to sneak into the organization and suck the energy out of everyone, leaving these lifeless corpses behind?

Frank knew a bit of his company's history. He knew that the original founder, Roy Fitzsimmons (who was now retired), had deep technical expertise and extensive professional training in their industry. He knew that Mr. Fitzsimmons was passionate about the company's pioneering technology. He had an exciting and powerful vision with an intense drive to blaze new pathways. This energy and excitement had attracted like-minded team members, customers, partners, and investors, and had fuelled their rapid early growth.

Over the next few days, Frank made a point of seeking out the company veterans to ask them about the culture and focus of the early days. He also reviewed some archival material on their first products, strategies, financial statements, correspondence, and the like. He learned that the company grew strongly on the strength of its technology. It was an exciting, fun place to work. But it struggled financially. Management systems and processes were weak or nonexistent. So costs were high. Error rates and rework were also high and Frank heard lots of "heroic recovery" stories of fixing up customer problems.

As Mr. Fitzsimmons neared retirement, he decided to hire a "professional manager" as president and CEO while he stepped back into the role of chairman. The new president imposed much-needed organization and order on the fledgling company. But, Frank knew, you can take any good idea too far. While the pendulum had been way over on the leadership side of the equation, the new president swung it sharply to the management side. Slowly the spirit and vitality was squeezed out of the company. The soft, intangible feelings of making a difference and being part of a meaningful cause were driven out by the drive to achieve hard results – goals, objectives, and the bottom line. Communications and meetings that were once full of exciting reports about new customers, innovative products developed on a shoe string, new market frontiers opening, and outstanding service delivered in extraordinarily tough circumstances were now filled with dry reports on progress to sales and profit goals, committee activities, strategies, budgeting, and business planning.

It became uninspiring and lifeless. The management imbalance dehumanized people and turned them into their roles. Expressions like "business is business" and "it's not personal, it's business" were heard more regularly. People became number crunchers, orders processors, product producers, sales pushers, researchers, technical problem solvers, managers, and budgeters. Their heart and soul were hung up in the closet with their overcoats and hats on the way in to work each morning. People went from being part of a cause that provided a paycheck to collecting a paycheck without a cause.

A hierarchy of Spirit and Meaning

"This dynamic of meaning making is, most researchers agree, the way resilient people build bridges from present-day hardships to a fuller, better constructed future. Those bridges make the present manageable, for lack of a better word, removing the sense that the present is overwhelming."

DIANE COUTU, SENIOR EDITOR AT *HARVARD BUSINESS REVIEW*, SPECIALIZING IN PSYCHOLOGY AND BUSINESS

Cultural transformation consultant Richard Barrett provides a useful model for categorizing levels of organizational spirit and meaning. Like Abraham Maslow's famous Hierarchy of Needs, Barrett's approach shows the progression from meeting basic needs toward self-actualization and making a bigger difference in this world:

1. **Survival consciousness:** Totally focused on profits. Autocratic and fear-driven.
2. **Relationship consciousness:** Benevolent dictatorship. Loyalty between team members is stronger than to the organization.
3. **Self-esteem consciousness:** Desire to be the biggest or best. Hierarchical power structure. Search for efficiency, productivity, quality, and excellence.
4. **Transformation:** Self-discovery, vision, mission, and values. Shift from control to trust, fear to truth, privilege to equality, and fragmentation to unity.
5. **Organization consciousness:** Release of innovation and creativity. Creating conditions for cohesion, community spirit, trust, diversity, and mutual accountability.
6. **Community consciousness:** Voluntary environmental and social audits. Support to local community. Search for long-term sustainability.
7. **Global/Society consciousness:** Contribution to solving social, human rights, and environment issues beyond local community. Focus on ethics. Search for truth and wisdom.

Barrett's model shows how leaders can move themselves, their teams, and their organizations beyond success to significance. Moving up this hierarchy taps into ever deeper levels of human spirit and meaning. Many managers are stuck in the first three levels. What's worse, they often use "leaderspeak" language from Levels 4 to 7. They confuse knowing with doing. For example, we have met many managers who have gone through the motions of "doing transformation" (Level 4) without transforming. So they "do their vision/values/purpose thing" while continuing to hold personal beliefs such as: people can't really be trusted; people need to be closely "snoopervised"; rank has it's privileges; and maintaining "departmental silos" (where everyone is isolated inside high walls in their own areas). This further "Dilbertizes" the workplace and often frustrates people in their organizations even more than if those managers just stayed in Levels 1 to 3 and defended that as the right place to be.

Richard Barrett analyzed the core ideology of the 18 visionary companies in James Collins and Jerry Porras' seminal study, *Built to Last*. These long-term success stories (average corporate lifespans of over 100 years and still leading their fields) achieved shareholder value 15 times greater than the general market's growth. Barrett found that these companies had progressed beyond "maximizing shareholder wealth" (from Levels 1 to 3) as a driving force for their goals and cultures. Most of their objectives and ideology aimed at Level 5 and beyond. He concluded that "[an] organization's performance is directly related to its ability to tap into its human potential. For the average person, work is one of the most important ways he or she gives expression to who they are, and find their fulfillment."

Barrett outlines the big leadership challenge on the horizon: "Successful business leaders of the 21st century will need to find a dynamic balance between the interests of the corporation, the interest of the workers and the interests of society as a whole. To achieve this goal they will need to take account of the shift in values taking place in society, and the growing demand for people to find meaning and purpose in their work."

Let's be Frank (III): Growing to the next level

Frank found that Richard Barrett's seven-level hierarchy provided a useful model for thinking about what was needed to bring spirit and meaning to his organization. Sitting in his study at home during one of his early-morning R & R (reflection and renewal) periods, he thought to himself, "I can see that I allowed myself to become a victim of our short-sighted management culture – both personally and professionally. Our company has been locked into the lower levels. At the beginning, we needed to focus on survival (Level 1), then build relationships (Level 2), and then become more efficient and productive (Level 3). The problem is we haven't moved up any further in the growth hierarchy. By failing to grow in spirit, our basic needs have stagnated into greed for both more money and power. It's never enough. We're all tuned into radio station WIFM – What's In it For Me. I need to find a way to help people through the transformation I've personally gone through (Level 4) and into the higher orders of spirit and meaning represented by Levels 5 to 7."

Frank focused on leading his division to higher levels of consciousness. From there he hoped to influence or inspire his peers, boss, and the rest of the company to evolve as well. Frank read books and searched the Internet using key phrases like "spirit in the workplace," "soulful leadership," and "culture change." He even took time off to attend an international conference on business and consciousness.

At that conference he participated in a workshop led by a very experienced and knowledgeable transformation consultant whose books he had read and admired. Frank peppered her with questions on the specifics of taking her noble and uplifting ideas, and applying them in his workplace. But all he seemed to get from her in reply were vague generalities. Sensing his frustration, she approached Frank after the session and said, "I'm sorry I wasn't able to give you the simple formula you were looking for. But attaining higher levels of being isn't a paint-by-numbers project. Part of it is about readiness. Some people and organizations are more ready then others for the transformation from 'what's-in-it-for-me' to 'what's-best-for-the-common/greater-good.' We must each find what works for our own unique personalities, corporate culture, and individual team members. It's like trying to find a path in a field of newly fallen snow. Once we walk across the field, we've discovered our path."

Finding your personal 'It'

In the 1991 movie "City Slickers," Billy Crystal plays the part of Mitch, a middle-aged man in crisis who has lost his direction. He and his friends journey to the Wild West to participate in a real cattle drive and search for the meaning of life. Jack Palance plays Curly, a crusty old cowhand whose job it is to baby-sit the city slickers along the dusty trail. In one memorable piece of dialog, Curly asks Mitch:

"You know what the secret of life is?"

"No, what?" Mitch responds.

Curly holds up his index finger. "This."

Mitch looks confused. "Your finger?"

"One thing. Just one thing." Curly growls. "You stick to that and everything else don't mean sh-t."

"That's great," Mitch replies, "but what's the one thing?"

Curly smiles. "That's what you've got to figure out."

In typical movie fashion, of course, Mitch solves his problems by gaining new perspectives on his life and knowing what changes he has to make. He's learned that "it" – the one thing – varies for each of us. As Mitch tells one of his fellow searchers, "It's something different for everybody. It's whatever is the most important for you."

Strong leaders are especially good at defining "it" for their team or organization. "It" often connects back to the organization or team's vision, values, and purpose – at the hub of the Leadership Wheel (see page 22). Keeping the team or organization centered is a core leadership function.

When people are proud of their work, they bind organizations together with a shared sense of spirit and meaning.

Connecting with Pride

It's easy to make a buck. It's a lot tougher to make a difference.

Tom Brokaw, network news anchor and journalist

A few years ago, we had a local company, Artistic Landscaping, do extensive work on our backyard with a new deck, waterfall and pond, stone work, and perennial gardens. We joked with the husband-and-wife owners (Pat and Juanita), and their crew, about Pat's fastidiousness. Every night before they left, the crew would tidy up and, across our back lawn, lay out their rakes, shovels, wheelbarrows, and other equipment in precise order according to the numbers stenciled on each piece. This type of care applied to every aspect of the business: Their equipment – including trucks, trailers, and "Bobcat" – all had matching company colors and logo. Everyone wore corporate T-shirts and shorts. The company's quality and service were superb. They fussed about every little detail. After a long day of work, Pat and Juanita would meet with us to review what had been done, address our concerns, respond to suggestions, and explain what would happen at the next stage. Their crew was polite and very respectful of our time, property, and just what we wanted in order to create our "backyard oasis."

Artistic Landscaping exhibited another key part of the "it" that fosters spirit and meaning and provides strong connectedness – pride. Everyone was very proud of their work and clearly wanted to produce the best they could each day.

Pride is a distinctive hallmark of strong leadership. Leaders who deeply connect people to their organization, its products or services, each other, customers, and other partners, cultivate an outstanding pride-of-craft and sense of ownership in many ways – both highly visible and subtle. These might include workplace cleanliness and orderliness, maintenance of equipment and tools, the condition (such as being kept nicely painted and clean) of vehicles or machines, or the quality and quantity of training. Frontline servers and producers are treated with dignity and respect as noble professionals making valuable contributions that make a difference.

During times of change, the organization's underlying values, past accomplishments, and heritage are honored and built upon – even if they are being shifted in radically new directions. The organization's identity or brand is strong and consistent both outside and inside the organization. It's an extension of the organization's "lived values" and strong leadership. Team members care strongly about the brand and the organization's reputation because they feel a profound sense of connection to it. They also feel close to the organization's customers and care deeply about serving them well.

Spirited cultures give a competitive edge

"Now we have results from a range of industries that link leadership to climate and to business performance, making it possible to quantify the hard difference for business performance made by something as soft as the 'feel' of a company."

DANIEL GOLEMAN, RICHARD BOYATZIS AND ANNIE MCKEE, *PRIMAL LEADERSHIP: REALIZING THE POWER OF EMOTIONAL INTELLIGENCE*

Southwest Airlines founder Herb Kelleher said, "It's the intangibles that are the hardest things for a competitor to imitate. You can get an airplane. You can get ticket-counter space; you can get baggage conveyors. But it is our *esprit de corps* – the culture, the spirit – that is truly our most valuable competitive asset."

Decades of research show just how right Kelleher is. An organization's culture is the key factor in its performance. A growing number of studies are showing that companies that have strong cultures – with a balanced focus on customers, people, and shareholders – while emphasizing continuous change and strong leadership, produce dramatically better results. High-performing cultures often generate revenue, profit, and investment returns that are hundreds of percent higher than average organizations.

Success Profiles studied over 600 businesses during an eight-year period to assess the impact of mission, vision, and guiding principles – the hub of organizational culture – on financial performance. Those companies who scored "Poor" (on defining and communicating their mission, vision and guiding principles) had an average profit per employee of $7,802, versus $27,401 for those companies with a rating of "Very Good."

Some managers have "done their leadership thing" and developed mission statements or snappy logos. I have a closet full of nice shirts from numerous management conferences, each adorned with logos and clever slogans. A few of the slogans were actually believed by the participants (at the time, anyway). But, sadly, most weren't. The catchphrase added a nice pizzazz to the conference, but it didn't express anything credible to the participants. The upbeat, gung-ho slogan didn't reflect the organization's culture and was soon snickered down or forgotten – until the planning committee started looking at next year's conference.

High-performance organizations pull together the intangible leadership principles that define their unique character and rally people around a deeper sense of purpose. These powerful feelings are made tangible through the strong implementation of management processes and systems that translate ideals into action. In many cases, a slogan or statement really captures the organization's culture or aspirations. It resonates with most people and articulates the deeper feelings they have. Or the phrase can provide a rallying cry for further cultural development. Here are some examples:

- A school bus company: "Carrying our nation's future."
- A financial services company: "Helping our clients build financial freedom and security."
- A municipal department: "Building and leaving a legacy for our children and grandchildren."
- A mining company: "Stewards of the earth's resources for the benefit of its people."
- An industrial accident prevention and safety association: "A world were risks are controlled because everyone believes that suffering and loss are morally, socially, and economically unacceptable."

Let's be Frank (IV): Snowballs, stones, and stories

Frank had a few ideas about how to strengthen his leadership and bring more spirit and meaning into the organization. But he felt that he needed the fresh and informed perspective that an outside expert could offer. So he hired Pat, a consultant, to provide an assessment. Pat conducted confidential interviews with Frank and with each of the managers on his team. He sat in on a few management meetings. Pat also ran some focus groups with frontline staff groups.

During their first feedback session, Pat asked Frank if he'd noticed how much sniping there was going on between his managers. "It's just good fun," Frank objected. "Yeah, often it is and that's great," Pat replied. "But it can also be like having a snowball fight. As long as the snowballs are soft and fluffy, everything's fine. Then someone throws a snowball with a stone inside, which hits you in the head. That person will often say, 'It was just in fun'. But that doesn't make the snowball hurt any less." Pat looked down at his notes and concluded, "There are a few stones and some rocks being thrown around your meeting rooms, offices, and halls. A number of people have told me privately how much some of these hurt. They are eroding the team's spirit. Also, a lot of the humor around here is pretty cynical, and nothing destroys team spirit faster than cynicism. Snide remarks, barbs, and pessimism are like an acid that corrodes deeper connectedness and meaningful workplaces."

Frank and Pat decided that the sniping problem was a good place to start reconnecting the team. In consultation with the managers, they agreed to set up a Sniping and Cynicism Rule: If any team member made a comment that sounded like a putdown, cheap shot, or cynical remark, the others would tap their glasses or cups with a pen. The offender would then be required to deposit two dollars in a pot set up for this purpose, the contents of which would be donated to a designated charity at the end of each quarter. (This strategy also prompted Frank to identify local charities and community projects that were of interest to people in the organization, and to provide them with support – both in allowing time off work and in donations of financial support.)

Frank's leadership plan to reconnect people focused on communication – holding "town hall" meetings in which he shared Pat's assessment report, discussed strengths, weaknesses, and improvement opportunities, asked for input and ideas, and got everyone involved in the improvement process. Frank also worked to develop his verbal communication skills. He became a corporate "storyteller," sharing with others what he had learned about the company's rich heritage and how previous leaders had dealt with many changes and crisis points.

All of us need to connect with something more important than our own personal success.

FROM ME TO WE

Joy can be real only if people look upon their life as a service, and have a definite object in life outside themselves and their personal happiness.

LEO TOLSTOY

There are two ways we can look at the types of corporate statements listed on page 144. The more pessimistic view – and, unfortunately, an accurate one in many cases – is that they have more to do with an organization's marketing strategy than its reality. But where such statements really do reflect the company's culture, they point to higher-order states of corporate consciousness. They show how these organizations have evolved beyond what's-in-it-for-me to how they can make a bigger difference in the world.

These are examples of what Charles Handy calls "an abundance of the 'E' factors, when 'E' stands for energy, enthusiasm, effort, excitement, excellence and so on." In his book *The Hungry Spirit: Beyond Capitalism – A Quest For Purpose in the Modern World*, he explains, "the talk is about 'we', not 'I', and there is a sense that the organization is on some sort of crusade, not just to make money, but something grander, something worthy of one's commitment, skills and time."

When companies make statements that are inconsistent with what people experience every day on the job, then cynicism deepens. However, where strong leaders help people to feel an emotional connection to the organization's deeper identity, brand, or promise, then commitment deepens. Acting on those powerful feeling of connectedness, people in these organizations work to reinforce the organization's ideals and keep the virtuous circle turning.

A key indicator of the health of an organization's culture – especially its connectedness – can be found in its internal communication patterns. Management consultant Ian Percy frames this well in his book, *Going Deep*: "Right now, your organization has exactly the kind of communication it deserves, be it good or bad. Communication is simply the testimony of the degree of unity your organization is experiencing. When an organization has real unity – that is, unity in body, mind and spirit – it does not have a 'communication problem'… the experience of unity is central to being spiritual. In other words, one major characteristic of a spiritually centered organization is that it enjoys and benefits from constant 'common-unity-cation.'"

Let's be Frank (V): Redefining the role of leadership

Some months after they had implemented the new leadership plan, Frank talked with Pat about how well the improvement process was going. He reported that energy and commitment levels around the organization were rising.

"We are starting to see a big drop in absenteeism, complaints, and service/quality problems," Frank enthused. "People are really getting into things around here. Yesterday, when I talked to Steph from accounting during their Hawaiian theme day, she had just come back from visiting a client. She went on and on about what a different place this was becoming. 'It's sure a lot more fun to come to work now,' she told me."

"There's just one thing," Frank continued. "I'm spending so much time out of my office now that I am getting less and less of my own work done." He nodded toward the large pile of files and papers in his in-box. "Last week my boss saw me in the parking lot and asked if I was taking more time off! Seems he had been trying to reach me and always found me out of my office."

Pat looked at Frank and asked, "What do you think your real leadership work is?"

"What do mean?"

"I mean, you have been turning around the spirit of your organization and bringing a deeper sense of meaning and fun to people here. That's leadership." He pointed to the stack of files. "Shouldn't you delegate and develop people to do that stuff?" Frank thought for a moment. "You're right. My work is caring for the context. My role is working *on* the business, not *in* the business. I need to explain that to my boss and help him see how the turnaround we're now producing here comes from leadership, not micromanagement. Perhaps I can even influence him to take a look at *his* leadership..."

ALL THAT WE CAN BE

Great teams are led by great coaches who inspire and assist each member in achieving his or her full potential.

GROWING AND DEVELOPING

A true Master is not the one with the most students, but one who creates the most Masters. A true leader is not the one with the most followers, but one who creates the most leaders.

NEALE DONALD WALSCH

Maybe it's just because I was raised on a farm, but whenever I hear managers use the term "head count" (and I hear it a lot), it grates on me like fingernails scratching a blackboard. When managers say things like "we've got to reduce our head count" or "what's the head count in your division?", I immediately think of cattle. In the community where I grew up, farmers would ask each other questions like "how many head are you milking?" when talking about cows in a dairy herd. People were never referred to this way.

Of course, some managers will argue that "head count" is just an expression – "mere words," they'll say. Sometimes that's true. But in my experience, these "mere words" often convey a deeper set of values about how people are viewed and treated in an organization. Despite all their pious declarations about the importance of people, leadership, and values, far too many managers treat people in their organizations with about as much care as they would attach to an inventory of office equipment. They are just one more set of assets to be managed. These just happen to be breathing and have skin wrapped around them.

Successful leaders understand the difference between things and people in an organization. They know that it's important to *manage* things, but that it's even more important to *lead* people. Leaders don't just mouth empty phrases like "people are our greatest resource"; they demonstrate by their *actions* that people – not strategy, products, plans, processes, or systems – are the most critical factor in an organization's performance. That's why leaders invest heavily in growing and developing people, while managers see people as objects to be commanded and controlled.

In his *Fortune* article "A New Way to Think about Employees," Thomas Stewart writes, "We should not confuse human beings with human capital at all. Surely people are not assets in the same way that their desks and chairs are assets, or that factories or bank balances are." Phrases like "head count" dehumanize and objectify people. We could really push this further and make the same argument for "human resources." Most of us want to be treated as a person, not a resource.

Managers who view "their people" as property are cold and dispassionate. In fact, they would make perfect donors for heart transplants – their hearts have had such little use!

Leaders work with people to discover where they are best able to thrive and succeed.

Growing Spaces

Treat people as if they were what they ought to be and you help them become what they are capable of being.

GOETHE

I enjoy perennial gardening in our yard. As I have tended our gardens over the years, I am continually struck by how some plants will do well in some locations and terribly elsewhere in the garden. Each spring and fall I move plants around to match their preferences for particular soil, wind, and sun conditions, as well as their proximity to other plants.

At times I have been pleasantly surprised by how some lackluster plants have suddenly thrived in a new location better suited to their needs. Since each perennial has a different bloom time and length, one of the gardening challenges is to keep color spread throughout the garden from early spring to late fall. It's one reason I never "cheat" by using annuals that bloom all summer long. A constant chore is cutting off old blooms to encourage new ones and pruning plants that are becoming overgrown.

Managers often use a "one size fits all" approach and try to "mass grow" people. Leaders work closely with their team members to customize their growth and development. Like a good gardener, leaders treat each person in their organization as an individual with his or her own unique aspirations, strengths, and characteristics. Leaders then work to put people in the best place for them to thrive and succeed. They mix and match team members to build a well-rounded team that can show its best colors according to the season – or is best suited to the current operating conditions of the organization or the team. Leaders tend to each person on their team and coach them to change habits or prune overgrown methods that may prevent further growth. They are consistently moving team members around to avoid overcrowding and to bring out the best in each person.

The fish-tank factor

If you buy a little goldfish and keep it in a small bowl it will remain no bigger than a few inches long. Move that same fish to a large aquarium and it will double or triple in size. Put the goldfish in a large pond and it can grow up to a foot long! The biggest factor that determines the size of the fish is the size of its environment. And so it is with people.

Managers see people as they are and treat them according to what they see. A manager would take a small goldfish and keep it in the little bowl because it would be inefficient and wasteful to put it in a larger environment. Leaders, on the other hand, see people as they could be. A leader takes a small goldfish and puts it in a larger tank because it would be ineffective and wasteful of the fish's potential to keep it in a confined environment.

Leaders provide a bigger environment by delegating autonomy. Strong leaders are strong coaches. They clarify performance targets, develop skills and abilities, reinforce progress, and build on strengths. Leaders consult, facilitate, counsel, and guide. They also confront when they feel someone is not living up to his or her potential.

Management (Small Fishbowls)	**Leadership (Large Fish Tanks)**
Commanding	Coaching
Solving problems	Enabling others to solve problems
Directing and Controlling	Teaching and Engaging
Seeing people as they are	Developing people into what they could be
Empowering	Partnering
Operating	Improving
Pushing	Pulling
Heroic Manager	Facilitative Leader
Quick fix to symptoms	Search for systemic root causes

Managers use position, leaders use persuasion.

POWER USAGE

The defining aspect of what we call 'civilization' is not art or architecture, fashion or furniture but how people with power deal with people without power.

NOAH BEN SHEA, POET AND SCHOLAR

Richard Boyatzis, one of the founders of competency theory and a professor at Case Western Reserve University reports, "From my research I'm left with the impression that half of the managers in organizations are decreasing value, not adding value." One of the reasons for this serious performance gap is that too many managers believe that their place on the organization chart gives them power. They are in control. They are the boss. Their attitude seems to be "I am really easy to get along with once you learn to do as I say."

I once had a recently laid-off manager tell me about the horrible, soul-destroying organization he had just left. They had a 50% turnover rate and were struggling to stay afloat in the highly competitive automotive parts industry. He said that behind closed doors, one of the CEO's favorite comments about the organization's people was "use them up and throw them away."

"Well," snarled the tough old sergeant to the bewildered private. "I suppose after you get discharged from the Army, you'll just be waiting for me to die so you can come and spit on my grave."

"Not me, Sarge!" the private replied. "Once I get out of the Army, I'm never going to stand in line again!"

"What's the difference between the Pope and my boss?"

"The Pope only expects you to kiss his ring."

Of course, a manager's position gives him or her rank. But authority and true power to lead can't be given or commanded. It can only be earned. As Margaret Thatcher, the former British Prime Minister once put it, "Being powerful is like being a lady. If you have to tell people you are, you aren't."

A big reason for the poor performance of so many teams and organizations is that they suffer from ineffective managers who subscribe to the old-fashioned model of the "tough, take-charge boss." Traditionally, such individuals often used command and control, bullying, intimidation, and "riding staff hard" to get the job done. Generations of managers yelled their way up the corporate ladder.

But the days of automatic deference to authority are long gone. We don't live in the world of might-is-right any more. Dictatorships are being replaced by democracies. Experts don't have as many answers as we once thought. We all have many more job or business options available to us. In today's workplace, a management style of pushing people around often pushes the highest performers right out the door.

During a workshop designed to identify Moose-on-the-Table issues (see page 102), a manager was surprised by the very clear and strong feedback he got from his organization that his management group was not behaving as a team. They contradicted each other, waged petty turf battles, and reinforced departmental silos. His response was like threatening to cut off an infected arm rather than then diagnosing and treating the cause of the infection. At their next management meeting, he read them the riot act. In a variation on the age-old bully boss tradition of firings-will-continue-until-morale-improves, he warned them, "If you don't behave as a team, I'll replace you with managers who will."

Heroes don't develop others

"There are incalculable resources in the human spirit, once it has been set free."

HUBERT HUMPHREY, FORMER U.S. VICE PRESIDENT

Remember the old television series, The Lone Ranger? A lot of traditional managers see themselves in a similarly heroic role. In the TV show, when the poor hapless townsfolk got themselves into big trouble, the Lone Ranger and his faithful sidekick would come riding over the hill. With the right degree of courage, wit, and cunning, he faced down the mean hombre or otherwise took care of the problem for the town. At the end of the nice, neat, half hour episode, our hero would leave the grateful townsfolk behind wondering, "Who was that masked man?"

The same spirit of rugged individualism runs deep within many of today's "heroic managers." They solve problems, take command, control and direct, occasionally empower team members, and are caught up in putting out daily operating fires. They are often overworked and a growing number are burning out. Managers often talk about their volume of email, voice mail, projects, meetings, and many hours worked. Is that bragging or complaining? One of the big reasons typical managers are caught up in their "busyness" cycle is because it makes them feel important. They are at the center of the action. They are making it happen. They get the adrenaline rush of urgent heroic problem-solving that saves the day for their poor hapless team.

Leaders spend much less time personally solving problems. They invest their time in making sure that the right problems are being solved. Here's how we might rewrite The Lone Ranger script for a leader rather than a heroic manager:

Scrooge would be proud...

"I used to be the Public Relations Coordinator and Editor for a local nonprofit organization... my grandmother became very ill. After a phone call from a family member I was told to come to her bedside, as death was imminent. I told my boss that I needed to leave for a family emergency and explained the situation and how close I was to my grandmother. My boss replied, 'Well, she's not dead yet, so I don't have to grant your leave.' And, I was told to complete my workday. Suffice to say I did not finish my workday."

MESSAGE POSTED ON WWW.BUSRESLAB.COM

Responding to the call for help, the Lone Ranger rides into town, gets down off his high horse, takes off his mask, and facilitates a process by which the townspeople solve the crisis for themselves. He gets to know the people and matches their strengths and abilities to established performance targets. After seeing them through the crisis, he rides out of town, with the townspeople saying, "Hey, we solved this ourselves."

When the next problem arose, the townspeople might still call for the Lone Ranger, but in an advisory capacity; they would be more likely to handle the crisis within the team. Each time they handled their own problems, they would increase their ability to identify and eliminate the root causes, their capacity to work as a team, and their level of confidence. Eventually the Lone Ranger and Tonto would join the lonely Maytag Repairman, flipping playing cards into their hats as they swap stories around the campfire.

Of course, the "leader version" of the Lone Ranger wouldn't make very good television. It's less dramatic and action packed. The hero doesn't save the day. Heading off problems and solving root causes leads to less pressure-packed "excitement." Getting teams to share the workload and become more self-sufficient reduces the short-term adrenaline rush. It totally shifts the team leader's role and focus.

The fact is that organizations need both management and leadership. Ultimately it depends on the situation. There are times when the manager needs to ride into town, take control, issue commands, and solve the problem immediately. Indeed, to do otherwise in such cases might be seen as an abdication of responsibility. But such actions are generally needed only as a short-term response in times of crisis. If managers stay in crisis mode continuously, they weaken their teams, increase their own workload, multiply dependence on them, kill commitment and ownership, and reduce partnering. Personal, team, and organization growth is stunted.

Our belief in people's abilities to grow and develop – or our lack of it – often becomes a self-fulfilling prophecy.

Great Expectations

Trust men and they will be true to you; treat them greatly and they will show themselves great.

Ralph Waldo Emerson

Heather and I have lived in over half a dozen homes since we married in 1977. Every neighborhood we've lived in has been full of kind, courteous and very thoughtful neighbors. There have been numerous parties, "newcomer clubs," casserole brigades, watching each other's homes, and the like. Heather is one of the kindest, most considerate human beings I know. She loves people and takes a deep interest in the lives and welfare of everyone she meets. Within weeks of moving into a new home she is organizing social or community events. She will drop everything to console someone in need or just be a good listening friend. One day, one of Heather's long-time friends said "you've lucked into a great neighborhood everywhere you've moved. We've never found a friendly neighborhood we've ever liked. Everyone is so cold and distant everywhere we go." Funny thing about Heather's luck, the more neighborly she is, the luckier she becomes in happening upon great neighborhoods.

An old adage asks, "How am I expected to soar with the eagles when I'm surrounded by a bunch of turkeys?" This is a common victim statement, often heard from underperforming managers. Leaders see people as they could be – as eagles in training. Managers simply see them as turkeys. Research shows that both get what they expect.

In his *Harvard Business Review* classic "Pygmalion in Management," J. Sterling Livingston draws upon the ancient Greek myth of Pygmalion, a sculptor who carved a statue of a beautiful woman that was later brought to life. George Bernard Shaw's play *Pygmalion* (which was the basis for "My Fair Lady") used a similar theme. In the play, Eliza Dolittle explains, "The difference between a flower girl and a lady is not how she behaves, but how she is treated."

Livingston presents a number of his own studies, as well as other research, to prove that "if a manager's expectations are high, productivity is likely to be excellent. If his expectations are low, productivity is likely to be poor."

What's now widely referred to as "The Pygmalion Effect" was pioneered by psychologist Robert Rosenthal at Harvard University. He told a group of students that high or low intelligence could be bred into laboratory rats through genetic manipulation. One group of students was given the "bright" rats. The other group of students was given the "dull" rats. When tested in their ability to navigate a maze, the bright rats dramatically outperformed the dull rats. What the students didn't know was that, in fact, there was no difference in the rats' intelligence levels. Both groups of rats were the same. The only variable was the expectations and emotional tone of the students handling the rats.

In his book, *Self-Fulfilling Prophecy,* Robert Tauber, a professor of education at The Behrend College of the Pennsylvania State University at Erie, compiled over 700 doctoral dissertations and countless journal articles on stereotyping, perception of social differences, race, gender, ethnicity, body features, age, socioeconomic levels, special needs, and other personal and situational factors showing "what we expect, all too often, is exactly what we get."

Robert Rosenthal later conducted the "Oak School experiment," which demonstrated how consistently held expectations become self-fulfilling prophecies. At Oak School, teachers were told that a group of students had been specially tested and were "intellectual bloomers." Although they might start off slowly, they could be expected to show remarkable gains throughout the school year. At the end of the year the "bloomers" showed a substantial jump in IQ and academic achievement. Teachers reported that they were more friendly, outgoing, and eager to learn than their peers. Of course, the teachers had been misled. This group had not been specially tested. They were randomly selected from student lists.

Set roles and goals. Build on strengths. Deal with poor performance. These are just some of the leadership strategies that help people grow.

The Coach's Playbook

You cannot teach a man anything; you can only help him to find it within himself.

GALILEO

Where do you find the highest levels of employee retention and productivity, customer satisfaction, and profitability? According to a major Gallup study (of more than 1.5 million employees across more than 87,000 divisions or work units), the answer can be found in how positively team members respond to twelve key indicators of the health of their workplace. These statements include factors such as recognition, clarity of goals, opportunities to use individual strengths, and having effective tools and equipment. Other indicators identify how much people feel cared for, whether their opinions count, personal growth opportunities, regular progress reviews, the team's commitment to doing quality work, and whether the organization's mission or purpose make the team member feel important. A more surprising factor that impacts the workplace is whether team members feel they have a best friend at work.

Curt Coffman, co-author of *First, Break all the Rules: What the World's Greatest Managers Do Differently* and *Follow this Path: How the World's Greatest Organizations Drive Growth by Unleashing Human Potential*, challenges the well-worn phrase "people are our greatest asset." Instead, the Gallup research shows the phrase is only partially correct: "The truly engaged and talented people that come to work every day are the real asset of your company....the best managers are persistent in creating environments where employees can strongly agree with the items in Gallup's employee engagement survey."

The Gallup research clearly shows that team member performance and productivity depends on growth and development that takes place at a "local" level – that is, the coaching provided by leaders who influence people directly. In other words, strong local leaders are able to build an island of excellence in a sea of mediocrity. Or a weak manager can produce very poor results despite a positive and successful organizational culture. As Gallup's John Thackray explains, the factors have "a common ingredient: remediability. [They] address a condition that is within the capacity of managers and workers to change together, as a team initiative. Fate and acts of God are sidelined."

Clarifying roles and goals

"Our chief want in life is somebody who can make us do what we can."
RALPH WALDO EMERSON

There's an old saying that teaches, "the clearer the target, the surer the aim." It's common sense: We can't achieve top-level performance if we're not clear what it looks like. But however obvious this critical coaching strategy may seem, many managers fail to practice it. Writing about this problem in the *Harvard Business Review*, in what they describe as "The Set-Up-To-Fail Syndrome," Jean-Francois Manzoni and Jean-Louis Barsoux report that "it is the bosses themselves – albeit unintentionally – who are frequently responsible for an employee's sub-par achievement." This is typically due to a lack of clarity in performance targets or standards, roles, and responsibilities. In our own consulting practice, we have also found that confusion in these areas is a primary cause of job dissatisfaction.

Effective coaches are masters at working with people to set the performance bar very high while aligning organizational, customer, and team needs with the individual's personal goals. While jobs may be shifting and roles evolving to meet changing conditions, a strong leader will get everyone involved in an ongoing process of redefining and resetting roles and goals. Strong leaders build upon successes and string together small wins to boost confidence about what can be achieved.

Building on strengths

"The test of a good manager is to make ordinary people perform better than what seems to be their capability, to bring out the strengths they have, and to use each employee's own internal desires to inspire them to greatness."
LUKE DE SADELEER AND JOSEPH SHERREN, *VITAMIN C FOR A HEALTHY WORKPLACE*

A water bearer in India had two pots attached to each end of a pole. He would sling the pole over his shoulders to carry water from the stream to his house every day. One of the pots was cracked and leaked water. The other one was perfect. One day the cracked pot spoke to the water bearer about its shame and apologized for dripping water while the other pot never lost a drop. The water bearer replied to the pot, "Yes, you are cracked and do not carry water as well your brother pot. But you have an ability that he does not have. Did you notice there were flowers on your side of the path, but not on the other pot's side? That's because I have always known about your flaw and took advantage of it. I planted flower seeds on your side of the path and every day while we walk back from the stream you have watered them."
ANON

Strong leaders know that we're all cracked pots. Perfect people are in very short supply! In fact, that may be just as well: As Abraham Lincoln once said, "It has been my experience that men who have no vices have very few virtues."

Dwelling on our own or other's weaknesses rarely improves them. And it sure doesn't do much for self-confidence, passion, or commitment. Like a good football coach who has different running backs for long- and short-yardage plays, a strong leader finds people whose strengths most closely match the requirements of the role (and whose weaknesses are less important) in a given situation. Rather than defining the ideal role and trying to find a perfect person to fit it, effective leaders find someone who meets most of the key criteria. He or she then tailors the responsibilities to align with the individual's strengths.

As shown in the Gallup study described on page 160, strong leaders give people a chance to do what they do best every day. Marcus Buckingham, co-author of *First, Break all the Rules* and *Now, Discover Your Strengths*, explains that great managers help people "develop their natural talents to such an extent that their areas of weakness become irrelevant... with the aim of elevating each person's performance to its highest possible levels... [strength-building] is what real development is all about."

Confronting poor performance

"He harms the good who spares the bad."

PUBLIUS SYRUS

When performance problems arise, they need to be confronted. Like porcupines in love, such discussions are painful for both parties. That's often why managers avoid them. Leaders, however, know that poor performance is like a highly contagious disease. The longer it goes unchecked, the more everyone suffers. Here are what some of the experts have to say about the subject:

Keeping poor performers means that development opportunities for promising employees get blocked, so those subordinates don't get developed, productivity and morale fall, good performers leave the company, the company attracts fewer 'A' players, and the whole miserable cycle keeps turning... Refusing to deal with underperformers not only makes your best employees unhappy, but it also makes them think the company is run by bozos... Successful companies deal with underperformers systematically, every day; unsuccessful companies don't."

GEOFFREY COLVIN, "MAKE SURE YOU CHOP THE DEAD WOOD," *FORTUNE*

I feel there is no greater disrespect you can do to a person than to let them hang out in a job where they are not respected by their peers, not viewed as successful, and probably losing their self-esteem. To do that under the guise of respect for people is, to me, ridiculous."

DEBRA DUNN, SENIOR EXECUTIVE, HEWLETT-PACKARD

Easing someone's path does not mean simply providing the path of least resistance. Sometimes the best way to help people is to hold them responsible; accepting no excuses can sometimes be the best kind of aid we can offer."

WILLIAM BENNETT, *THE MORAL COMPASS*

Servant-leadership

"If a would-be leader wants glamour, he should try acting in the movies. However, if he in fact wants to make a consequential impact on a cause or an organization, he needs to roll up his sleeves and be prepared to perform a series of grungy chores which are putatively beneath him, and for which he'll never receive recognition or credit, but by virtue of which his lieutenants will be inspired and enabled to achieve great things."

STEVEN B. SAMPLE, PRESIDENT OF THE UNIVERSITY OF SOUTHERN CALIFORNIA, *THE CONTRARIAN'S GUIDE TO LEADERSHIP*

So much of what a manager does makes it difficult for people to get their work done. "I am from head office and I am here to help you" sends the snicker meter over the red line in many organizations. Too often managers have made it harder for people on the front-lines to get their job done. Strong coaches start by building agreement or buy-in to roles and goals. Then they flip things around and serve their teams and organizations.

At a technical services company a manager declared a series of "junk days" for the technicians in the field. He pulled together a group of internal and external suppliers of the equipment the technicians were using and took them out on tour. He invited technicians to attend the meeting in a local hotel room and bring out all their defective equipment along with their work-around-strategies. The internal and external suppliers were told that they were there only to listen and learn. They were not to rationalize, defend, excuse, or explain. They were to speak only with questions for clarity. As the tour moved from city to city, the manager and the suppliers kept careful notes on the trends emerging and the many innovative solutions they encountered. At the end of the tour, decisions were made, new prototypes developed, and procedures changed. They then went back out on tour to get reactions and make further modifications. The result was a surge in morale, productivity, and effectiveness of the technicians.

We can't grow and develop if no one tells us how we're doing.

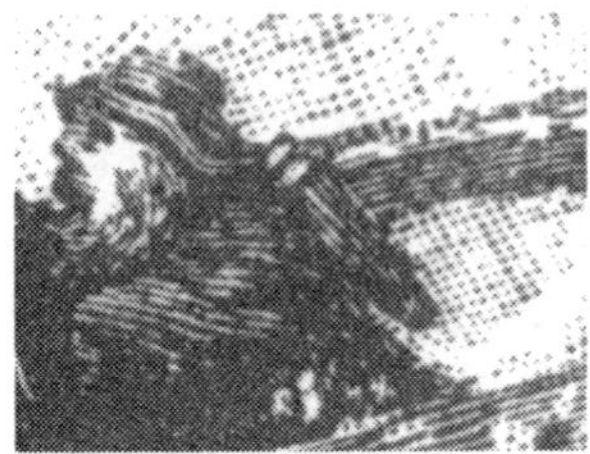

GIVING GOOD FEEDBACK

Effective leaders are effective communicators. And part of this skill is the ability to deliver useful feedback. Good feedback benefits both the giver and receiver. It nourishes growth and development. Without it, the leader-as-coach is unable to clarify performance targets, develop skills and abilities, reinforce progress, or build on strengths. Strong, relevant, and useful feedback shows how much leaders care about the growth of people on their team.

In their book *Vitamin C for a Healthy Workplace,* Luke De Sadeleer and Joe Sherren offer the following useful tips for giving good feedback:

It is descriptive rather than evaluative. By describing one's own reaction, it leaves the individual free to use it or not as they see fit. By avoiding evaluative language, the manager reduces the need for the individual to react defensively.

It is specific rather then general. If a manager tells an employee that they are "dominating," it will probably not be as useful to him or her as to be told that "just now when we were discussing the issue, you did not listen to what others said and I felt forced to accept your arguments or face attack from you."

It takes into account the needs of both the receiver and giver of feedback. Feedback can be destructive when it serves only one's own needs and fails to consider the needs of the person on the receiving end.

It is directed toward behavior that the receiver can do something about. Frustration is only increased when a person is reminded of some shortcoming over which they have no control.

It is well timed. In general, feedback is most useful at the earliest opportunity after the given behavior. This depends, of course, on the person's readiness to hear it, along with such variables as support available from others.

It is checked to insure clear communication. One way of checking for clear communication is to have the receiver try to rephrase the feedback he/she received to see if it corresponds to what the sender had in mind.

It is checked for accuracy. When feedback is given in a training group, both giver and receiver have an opportunity to check, with others in the group, the accuracy of the feedback. Within the group it's easier to determine if the feedback is only one person's impression or an impression shared by others.

Asking and listening

"Empathic (from empathy) listening gets inside another person's frame of reference. You look out through it, you see the world the way they see the world, you understand their paradigm, you understand how they feel...you're listening to understand."

STEPHEN COVEY, *THE SEVEN HABITS OF HIGHLY EFFECTIVE PEOPLE*

There are many factors that differentiate management and leadership. The ability to ask questions – and listen attentively to the answers – is one of them. Managers tell. They would rather be wrong than be quiet. Leaders listen. They know that growing and developing people is impossible without listening.

Asking and listening are fundamental to leadership. They are learnable skills. Whether we choose to develop them or not depends upon our values. Do we really care about the people we lead? Do we really think they have something useful to say? Are their feelings and issues misguided and petty or do they really matter to us? Are their attitudes something to be adjusted rather than probed for underlying improvement opportunities? Do we believe that customers' perceptions are to be changed rather than better understood and learned from? Do we often see internal or external partners (such as distributors, other agencies or departments, and suppliers) as whiners who just don't get it? As Winston Churchill put it, "courage is what it takes to stand up and speak. Courage is also what it takes to sit down and listen."

Recognize. Appreciate. Celebrate.
These are essential to encouraging growth and development.

Cheer Leaders

I have yet to find the man, however exalted his station, who did not do better work and put forth greater effort under a spirit of approval, than under a spirit of criticism.

Charles Schwab, legendary steel industry pioneer

It has been said that there are only two types of people who thrive on being recognized for their achievements: men and woman. (I guess that covers most of us!) Reflecting on a life of pioneering work, 19th-century American philosopher and psychologist William James said, "I now perceive one immense omission in my psychology – the deepest principle of human nature is the craving to be appreciated."

Effective leaders understand the power of sincere recognition, genuine appreciation, and celebration. These are what provide the atmosphere of encouragement that develops confidence and builds on strengths. This encouragement needn't come from the leader. It can be just as meaningful coming from peers, customers, team members, and other partners. But it's the leader who sets the emotional tone and atmosphere for recognition, appreciation and celebration in his or her organization.

Recognition, appreciation, and celebration continually show up near the top of most lists of motivational factors. In an article entitled "Rethinking Rewards," published in the *Harvard Business Review*, Andrew Lebby of The Performance Group reports, "Year after year we ask employees what motivates them, and year after year they reply (in order of priority):

1. A sense of accomplishment in performing the work itself
2. Recognition from peers and top management
3. Career advancement
4. Management support
5. Salary

Coaches show how much they *really* care

"All leadership is appreciative leadership. It's the capacity to see the best in the world around us, in our colleagues, and in the groups we are trying to lead."

DAVID COOPERRIDER, PROFESSOR, CASE WESTERN RESERVE UNIVERSITY

Most of us know intuitively whether someone is being a genuine leader, or is simply "doing their leadership thing." One of the major indicators is how much we feel that person cares about us and our opinions. In my experience, there are hundreds of little ways to tell how much managers care about the people in their organization. Do they use disparaging or objectifying language? Do they involve people in decisions which affect them? Do they try to make the workplace as healthy, safe, and pleasant as possible? Do they ensure that managers are well trained and held accountable for the leadership they provide? Do they openly share "confidential" information? Do they actively practice servant-leadership? Do they individualize rather than generalize? Finally – and this is one of the biggies – do managers ask for, carefully listen to, and act on input from everyone throughout their organization?

Too often managers think they're showing that they care by giving people patronizing pats on the head. These may take the form of goodies such as gifts, parties, long-service trinkets, trivial newsletters, or "royal visits" (occasional "touring of the troops" with much bowing and scraping). Not that these things are necessarily bad. Like anything, they are neither bad nor good in themselves, but in how they're used. When they substitute for treating people as respected and highly valuable partners, they increase cynicism and widen the we/they gap between management and people on the frontlines.

Top coaches draw top talent

One study of U.S. business school graduates shows that a growing number – it's now over half – are turning down higher-paying jobs for those that offer more room for personal growth. But too often personal growth is left completely up to the individual. Many organizations do a poor job of helping people grow. In a survey of 13,000 managers, only 3% strongly agreed that their companies were good at developing people!

Conventional wisdom is that management is getting things done through people. Strong leaders do that well. But they go further. Strong leaders coach and develop people through their work. Sometimes that means helping people do what they don't want to do so they can be the person they want to be.

Reflecting and renewing

"Fully 90% of managers squander their time in all sorts of ineffective activities... the smallest proportion of managers we studied – around 10% – were both highly energetic and highly focused. Not only do such managers put in more effort than their counterparts, but they also achieve critical, long-term goals more often... spend their time in a committed, purposeful, and reflective manner."

HEIKE BRUCH AND SUMANTRA GHOSHAL, "BEWARE THE BUSY MANAGER"

Many centuries ago there was a vast wilderness dividing two friendly nations. Caravans of traders traveled a rough highway through the sandy and rocky wastelands. It was a long and dangerous journey where animals and people often ran out of precious water and perished. One day, a traveler named Ephram got lost and wandered many miles off the beaten path through rocks, thorns, and barren desert that made the regular route seem like a stroll down a country lane. Confused and near death from thirst, he stumbled into a cave. As he went further into its cool and inviting depths, Ephram discovered a large pool of clear, cold water created by an underground spring. As he drank deeply and bathed in its refreshing waters, Ephram's failing eyesight (he had gone almost blind in the last few years) and pronounced limp were healed. When Ephram found his way back to the main road, word of the cavern and its miraculous waters spread quickly through the caravans. Although it was a two-day journey from the main route, Ephram's Cavern quickly became a life-saving stop for all convoys down through the years. Weary travelers were refreshed and rejuvenated. Travelers continued their long journey with renewed vigor and energy. The caverns became a major factor in the growing size and frequency of caravans that traveled through the immense wilderness.

As the years passed and travel experience grew, caravans became better equipped and able to go longer and longer distances without stopping. As trade between the two nations grew, so did the competition. Bigger and faster caravans began to rush right past the long and difficult road leading off to the distant, magical waters of Ephram's Cavern. Those travelers that did go to the caverns arrived at their destination days later than their harried competitors. But they were much healthier and their energy levels were higher. In the weeks and months of frantic trading activity that followed, those called the Ephram Travelers were less stressed, more focused, and used their time more wisely than their competitors. As a result, they finished their trading and left a few days earlier than the others. On the return trip, the Ephram Travelers once again made the long and difficult trek to the caverns. There they rejuvenated themselves and the beasts of burden carrying the heavy payloads to sell in their homelands. Since their harried competitors were already a few days behind, they again rushed past the cavern road to get home before the Ephram Travelers had commanded all the highest prices for the fine goods brought back from foreign lands.

Very often we find that managers and their teams are so busy working *in* the business that they have little time to work *on* the business. Meetings, deadlines, full email in-boxes, phone calls – comprised mostly of operational activities – suck up huge amounts of time and energy. We've often tried to work with such ineffective managers to set up training workshops and off-site planning retreats. But they are typically too busy fighting fires to spend time on any prevention strategies. As they work ever harder, the fires burn ever bigger. Too often this leads to burned-out managers, demoralized frontline staff, and slipping performance.

Strong leaders who are effective coaches know the value of R & R (reflection and renewal). They periodically pull themselves and their teams back from daily work in operations to work on themselves. They are constantly asking questions like "what should we keep doing, stop doing, and start doing to be more effective?" Coaches keep the fires under control by getting everyone involved in looking at underlying root causes and developing prevention strategies. This leads to renewed energy, clearer focus, and increased performance.

GO TEAM, GO

Leaders work from the inside, inspiring people to motivate themselves.

MOBILIZING AND ENERGIZING

Drawing energy out of people – or maybe a better way to say it is helping them to draw it out of themselves – and using that to help organizations leap and maneuver is going to be the critical leadership challenge.

JOHN KOTTER, LEADERSHIP AUTHOR AND HARVARD BUSINESS SCHOOL PROFESSOR

In The CLEMMER Group's training and consulting work we're frequently asked how to motivate, renew or revitalize people throughout the organization. A typical case was one where we were working with a manager who complained bitterly about "the declining work ethic" and how nobody took pride in his or her work any more. Like so many others in his position, he was searching for the "motivational magic button." He wanted to find some program or technique that would recharge the batteries of the people in his organization. He had tried a "sloganeering" campaign to get morale and service levels up. And to his credit, he had put together a well-managed internal communications program – including videos, newsletters and snappy slogans on coffee cups and T-shirts. But whatever effects it had were short-lived: In a few weeks, service quickly returned to its former mediocre level.

In the face of external changes and challenges, declining morale is a common problem in organizations today. All too often the result is that people effectively quit their jobs – even though they're still coming in to work every day.

Many organizations devote a lot of time and energy in search of the motivational Holy Grail. But such efforts typically end up treating the symptoms rather than root causes. If a manager really wants to find the reasons for plummeting morale and motivation, he or she needs to take a look in the mirror. W. Edwards Deming, the statistician and quality improvement guru credited with reviving Japanese (and, later, North American) production methods, points to a common cause of the problem: "The supposition is prevalent the world over that there would be no problems in production or in service if only our production workers would do their jobs in the way they were taught. Pleasant dreams. The workers are handicapped by the system, and the system belongs to management."

Motivation is an inside job. A manager can't singlehandedly motivate people, just as a gardener can't force plants to grow. Believing that we have the power to motivate other people is a common conceit – and any attempts to do so are rightly seen as manipulative. Strong leaders, on the other hand, recognize that their role is to create the conditions that lead to self-motivation.

The conditions affecting morale and motivation are varied and complex. When we conduct workshops or give presentations around the timeless principles in our Leadership Wheel (see page 22), we generally leave the principle of Mobilizing and Energizing until the end. That's because the degree of energy – or how mobilized people are – in a team or organization is the result of the other leadership principles. Leaders can do a number of things to mobilize and energize, but unless the other leadership principles are well established, such efforts will often appear manipulative and do more harm than good.

It's about more than money.

THE MOTIVATION MYTH

People do work for money – but they work even more for meaning in their lives. In fact, they work to have fun. Companies that ignore this fact are essentially bribing their employees and will pay the price in a lack of loyalty and commitment.

JEFFREY PFEFFER, "SIX DANGEROUS MYTHS ABOUT PAY," *HARVARD BUSINESS REVIEW*

We've known for decades that money doesn't motivate most people to higher levels of performance. In his seminal 1959 book, *The Motivation to Work*, Frederick Herzberg identified money as a "hygiene factor." If we feel we're not fairly compensated, lack of money can de-motivate. But once we feel we're treated fairly, the promise of more money doesn't sustain higher energy and mobilize inspired performance.

Numerous studies over the last few decades have shown that when it comes to understanding what really energizes and mobilizes, there's a huge we/they gap between managers and frontline people. For example, in an article entitled "Mastering the ABCs of Organizations," John R. Throop cites a study of computer programmers who were asked to identify the top 10 factors that provided the highest degree of motivation in their jobs. The programmers' top three were: full appreciation for work done; feeling that they were in on things; and, sympathetic help with personnel problems. The programmers' managers, when asked what these factors would be, predicted rather different priorities: wages, working conditions, and fair discipline.

When confronting morale problems, managers will often succumb to the Victimitis virus and blame the declining work ethic, attitudes of entitlement, softening values, the welfare state, or any number of societal factors. But these factors – which are mostly about doing the least work for the most money – are more imagined than real. Studies show that people's real needs are much less mercenary than most managers believe. People want to take pride in their work, belong to a winning team, and be part of an organization they can believe in. In fact, the morale crisis so prevalent in organizations today is primarily the result of disappointment in these needs not being met.

Ultimately, the problem is a leadership vacuum. The hand-wringing, teeth-gnashing managers, frustrated by their organizational energy crisis, often ask "why don't people want to work any more?" But that's the wrong question, based on the wrong assumptions. The question to ask – with a long gaze in the leadership mirror – is, "why don't people want to work *here*."

Managers try to motivate. Leaders inspire. Managers try to understand how to motivate people. Leaders try to understand why people aren't feeling motivated. Managers try to add more drivers to increase mobilization and energy. Leaders try to identify, prioritize, and remove the biggest resistors.

Leaders energize people by working for them.

Servant-Leadership

People are not "things" to be manipulated, labeled, boxed, bought, and sold. Above all else, they are not "human resource"... we must examine the concept of leading and following with new eyes. We must examine the concept of superior and subordinate with increasing skepticism.

Dee Hock, developer of VISA

Jet fighter pilot, Fortune 500 executive, and author of *Love and Profit: The Art of Caring Leadership,* James Autry explains the fundamental values of a strong servant-leader who facilitates the removal of barriers to higher performance: "As soon as I fulfill that expectation that I'm going to be 'Big Daddy,' I'm going to make a pronouncement and they're going to do it – I've destroyed any possibility to learn something from them and to recognize their own power, which is their knowledge and their skill, and which is real empowerment. Empowerment is not about 'I take some of my power and give it to you.' That's the myth. Real empowerment is recognizing that you, by your skill, your knowledge, your commitment, you already have power. What I'm trying to do is take off the leashes that I've put on."

In the 1970s, Robert Greenleaf – a retired AT&T executive and a lecturer at MIT, Harvard, and other universities – wrote a series of articles and a book entitled, *Servant-Leadership: A Journey into Legitimate Power and Greatness.* Since his death in 1990, Greenleaf's work and core philosophies have been spreading through continued book sales and the Greenleaf Center for Servant-Leadership (www.greenleaf.org). The Center's current CEO, Larry Spears, says that "the number of people who are familiar with the servant as leader idea and who are committed to it has grown to a critical mass; we are now witnessing the emergence of servant-leadership as a burgeoning social movement."

"Many are still locked into this idea that an organization is accurately reflected in the organizational chart, that top management somehow sits on the top... we claim that organizations are built on knowledge work today, and yet we still draw on these charts. Let me ask you, where do the knowledge workers go on the charts? They're at the bottom. Isn't that ridiculous? If the competitive advantage of an organization today is based on its knowledge workers, then why in the world would they be on the bottom?"

HENRY MINTZBERG, AUTHOR AND PROFESSOR

Spears goes on to provide the following definition of servant-leadership: "In all of his writings, Greenleaf discusses the need for a new kind of leadership model, one which puts serving others, including employees, customers, and community as the number one priority. The central definition of servant-leadership begins with the natural feeling that one wants to serve, to serve first. Then conscious choice brings one to aspire to lead. The difference manifests itself in the care taken by the servant – first to make sure that other people's highest priority needs are being served."

Far too many managers dismiss the frustrations of people in their organization as nothing but bitching, moaning, and petty gripes. "We don't need a bitch session" is how managers often shut down opportunities people might take to air their problems and grievances. Meanwhile, those same managers will go on to seek ways to "manage change," "motivate," or otherwise engage people in the organization. Somehow they expect frontline people to be interested in management issues even though the managers do not reciprocate by taking an interest in the issues that matter to frontline people. These managers don't want to be servant leaders, they want to be rulers. They don't get the connection between how caring for and serving frontline people mobilizes them to care for and serve the organization and its customers.

Servant-leaders remove the things that drain energy

When I first met Chris, he had been promoted to manager of field operations with a region of a few hundred people. Morale was as low as the unit's productivity and customer service. People were discouraged, turned off, and starting to fear for their jobs. Chris had to get everyone reenergized and reengaged in the business. We had been working with Chris' organization in a leadership development program. The concept of servant-leadership really clicked for Chris. He saw that the large "We-They Gap" between management and frontline people could be reduced by identifying and addressing their issues and concerns.

I told Chris about General Electric's famous "Workout Process," another client's innovative "Dumb Rules and Forms Committee," and a foundry's very successful "Barrier Removal Sessions." Chris was inspired to do something similar. This began with a series of meetings across the region with frontline field and support staff. In each session Chris briefly outlined the management team's vision for the region, the potential that Chris knew existed, the rich heritage of this successful company, as well as his desire to engage everyone in making the region more successful and a much more fulfilling place to work. Chris put one question on the top of a blank flipchart page: "What's the dumbest thing we do around here?"

At first there was little response. Most people didn't believe Chris was serious. When they tentatively began to bring out issues, Chris responded non-defensively, probed further, and wrote down all comments. So they began to dump out all their frustrations. The air was charged with emotion and anger. During a break, one of the managers on Chris' team privately bemoaned that the session was turning negative. Chris quickly corrected his perception. "There is energy here. That's very positive. These people care. They have been frustrated and losing hope. I think we've caught them just in time before apathy set in. We now need to harness and redirect that energy."

The list went on to fill many flipchart pages. Chris then worked with the group to cluster the list down to about six or seven major groupings. Chris then used a voting process to let people select what they considered to be the biggest issues that needed to be addressed. Once these were identified, Chris gathered suggestions on how to deal with them. The most obvious bonehead things that needed fixing right away were decided on the spot. Other issues needed more study or Chris needed to visit the other groups to see how common a problem it was.

A few months later, Chris came back through the region and met with each group again. Chris reported on which Dumb Things had been eliminated, updated progress on the bigger issues, and invited more ideas and input. The atmosphere was much more positively energized than the first time around. People began volunteering numerous things they could do to improve the organization or their workplace. These sessions continued and became an ongoing series of meetings that lay at the heart of a major turnaround in the region. Productivity, quality, customer service, and morale soared.

Working together generates a special kind of energy.

THE POWER OF TEAMS

"When I was a kid, I often wasn't the best player on the team. And when I got to GE, I wasn't always the smartest guy in the room. But I always looked to find the best – people smarter than me. Once I did that, they would take care of the rest. Building their own teams with the best. Every day, I fought to field the very best team. I always believed that was the way to win."

JACK WELCH, FORMER CHAIRMAN AND CEO, GENERAL ELECTRIC

Teamwork allows average people to achieve above-average results. That's highly energizing. Strong teams are full of turned-on people who are highly mobilized to keep performing at their full potential.

Research shows that teamwork is much more effective than individual effort. As the Japanese proverb teaches, "none of us is as smart as all of us." One study by the Employment Policy Foundation, a Washington think-tank, found that companies extensively using teams see their productivity jump 18 to 25 percent. Numerous studies and team development exercises continually prove that groups outperform individuals. Anyone who's ever

Effective teams huddle together

In Antarctica, Emperor penguins walk miles inland to court, mate, and raise their young. The males stay on the ice to incubate the egg, enduring a four-month period in which they go without a single meal. This is done in the Antarctic winter so the chick will be born in the "summer" months. They must survive temperatures approaching 100 below zero and blizzards with winds of 160 mph.

To cope with this, thousands of penguins huddle together in a huge group, as many as 10 per square yard. On windy days, the penguins on the windward edge block the cold from those in the center and leeward side. Each penguin takes its turn on the windward edge of the group before shuffling down the flanks of the huddle to rejoin it on the leeward side. They follow one another in a continuous procession, passing through the warm center and eventually returning back to the windward edge. During a blizzard, the huddle can move as much as 100 yards a day.

This kind of teamwork can't function with individualistic heroes. In fact, if some of the penguins decided to "tough it out" on the cold side, they would eventually die from exposure, thereby reducing the size of the group and the collective amount of heat generated. As the group got smaller, each remaining penguin would have to take more of the cold, thus reducing the chance they would survive. So heroes, in this case at least, can actually be dangerous. The greatest penguin success comes from everyone taking a little cold and warming back up.

MR PER, AMERICA'S CONFIDENCE COACH™

played a trivia game that allows group discussion before giving a final answer knows that. The ability to develop and lead effective teams is becoming a critical leadership competency as many organizations continue their sharp cultural shift to higher involvement and engagement of everyone at all levels.

Most managers have experienced the power of teams in some way. That's why so many have tried to organize teams and build teamwork. But calling a group of people a team doesn't make them one. Without strong team leadership, many groups don't become teams. It takes a lot more than posters on the wall with teamwork slogans to produce a team. Harvard's Chris Argyis has observed that you can put together a group of people with individual IQs of 130 and, without effective team leadership, they'll end up with a collective IQ of about 65.

In my consulting experience, I find that conventional "team-building exercises" rarely create strong teams. Scaling walls, participating in outdoor adventures, or playing games together can be lots of fun. But strong and lasting teamwork comes from getting a team to pull together around an issue or task that's key to the group's success. Focusing on results, high-performing teams can then identify the stepping stones (and stumbling blocks) to making the teams effective. While I will admit to a little bias on this point, I find that management teams often need an outside facilitator to keep them focused, break old group habits, and move the team to its next performance level.

Building high-performance teams

> *"When people experience the wholeness of their system, something happens to bring out the best in our capacity. It's like when the astronauts for the first time saw the planet from a distance: what happened was instant global consciousness and it changed the lives of those astronauts. The same things happen in organizational life to the extent that we can capitalize on this principle of wholeness."*
>
> DAVID COOPERRIDER, PROFESSOR, CASE WESTERN RESERVE UNIVERSITY

What does it take to transform groups into high-performance teams? Here are some of the key factors:

- **A well trained and skilled team leader**. The clearest differentiator between a group manager and a team leader is how well meetings are run. Most people hate meetings because they are too often a boring waste of time. Effective leaders run disciplined meetings that involve and engage participants and produce clear action plans with strong follow-through.

- **Facilitative leadership**. In *The Tao of Leadership*, John Heider adapts Lao Tzu's ancient wisdom to team leadership: "Your job is to facilitate and illuminate what is happening. Interfere as little as possible. Interference, however brilliant, creates a dependency on the leader. The fewer rules the better. Rules reduce freedom and responsibility. Enforcement of rules is coercive and manipulative, which diminishes spontaneity and absorbs group energy. The more coercive you are, the more resistant the group will become. Your manipulations will only breed evasions. Every law creates an outlaw. This is no way to run a group."

Giants stand together

Redwoods are the tallest of all trees, growing to almost 400 feet in height. To keep from falling over, you might expect redwoods to be anchored by very deep roots. Yet their roots are actually quite shallow, at times only 12 feet deep. How do these trees keep standing in the wind? While their roots are shallow, they are also very widely spread out. More importantly, redwoods grow very closely together, with the result that their wide roots intertwine and support one another. In fact, were it not for this support, redwoods would be physically incapable of standing against the elements.

MR PER, AMERICA'S CONFIDENCE COACH™

- **Seeing the big picture.** The old adage teaches that "it's hard to see the picture when you're inside the frame." It's hard for many team members to get excited about the work they are doing if they don't see how it fits together or if they don't feel like what they're doing matters all that much. We've seen many teams dramatically notch up their performance once a strong leader has shown them just how what they do plays an important part in a much bigger effort.

- **Strong feedback and learning loops.** Effective teams step back periodically to review their progress. They look at what's working and what isn't. They adjust course accordingly. Strong team leaders move beyond building a team of champions to building a championship team. High-performance teams work *on* the team as well as *in* the team. They regularly ask themselves, "What should we keep doing, stop doing, and start doing?" to become ever more effective.

- **Balanced for strengths**. Strong leaders add people to the team for their strengths, not for their absence of weakness. The leader then aligns those strengths to provide a diverse, well balanced team. (Of course, the weaknesses that come with the strengths can make for rocky rides!) Leading a diverse team takes confidence and strong facilitation skills.

- **Clear roles and goals**. Members of effective teams know where they fit and how they can make the biggest contributions to the team. The team has a disciplined process for reviewing and resetting priorities at the speed of change.

- **High Emotional Intelligence**. Researchers and management specialists Vanessa Urch Druskat and Steven Wolff report that "individual emotional intelligence has a group analog, and it is just as critical to a group's effectiveness. Teams can develop greater emotional intelligence and, in so doing, boost their overall performance." Another study of 62 management teams found that the more positive the mood, the more they cooperated and worked together. Not surprisingly, there was a direct correlation between cooperation and business results.

- **Strong laughter index**. Effective teams have fun. They care deeply about their work – but without taking themselves too seriously. Humor is clean and free of sniping, putdowns, sarcasm, and ridicule.

When we celebrate people's successes, they're inspired to keep succeeding.

RECHARGING WITH RECOGNITION

Motivation and inspiration energize people, not by pushing them in the right direction as control mechanisms do but by satisfying basic human needs for achievement, a sense of belonging, recognition, self-esteem, a feeling of control over one's life, and the ability to live up to one's ideals. Such feelings touch us deeply and elicit a powerful response.

JOHN KOTTER, "WHAT LEADERS REALLY DO," *HARVARD BUSINESS REVIEW*

Most of us have experienced the incredible energy of getting recognition or appreciation from people whose opinions we respect. We cherish notes, cards, letters, awards, trophies, or the warm afterglow of a compliment.

Still, the fact is that many managers fail to see the value of expressing such appreciation – despite the mountains of research on the energizing power of recognition, and

Jake, a circus owner, walked into a bar and saw a crowd gathered around a table. On the table was an overturned pot with a duck doing a lively dance on top of it. Jake immediately saw the huge potential of this act. He did some wheeling and dealing with the bar owner and finally agree to buy the duck and pot for $10,000.

Three days later Jake stormed furiously back into the bar with the duck and pot. "I put the pot down in front of a large audience and put the duck on it. It just sat there and wouldn't dance a single step! I demand my money back!"

The bar owner replied, "Did you light the candle under the pot?"

Moral: Managers try to light a fire under people. Leaders stoke the fire within.

despite experiences of having seen team members mobilized by feelings of success. Not surprisingly, one of the biggest complaints we hear from people in the workplace is that they don't get recognition and appreciation from their boss. They feel like a piece of furniture. It's a huge contributor to declining levels of morale and self-motivation. Studies show it's also one of the single biggest reasons why people leave an organization to work elsewhere.

There are many reasons why managers fail to provide the recognition that they should. Sometimes it's a matter of good intentions that don't get translated into actions. They may feel great about a team member's contribution. They might even praise that person to others. But they never get around to showing him or her just how much they appreciate and value that team member.

In other cases, managers actually do try to express their appreciation, but don't do it effectively. Common problems here include the following:

- Obvious flattery or exaggerated praise
- A prelude or "cushion" to criticism
- Paternalistic tone
- Not timely (for example, weeks or months after the event)
- Focuses primarily on top performers, excluding others
- Impersonal, phrased in generalities and platitudes

Meaningful appreciations

"There is an implicit, and I think wrong, assumption coming out of economics that you have to pay people a lot to get them to work. I think people have to feel that they are rewarded, recognized and appreciated in a broadly defined way. Simply relying on money to do that is nonsense."

CHARLES O'REILLY III, AUTHOR AND PROFESSOR, STANFORD UNIVERSITY

Where there's a will there's a way. A leader who really values the people in his or her organization will be constantly showing it through some formal programs and lots of informal gestures. The following provides some ways we've seen over the years for leaders to recognize, celebrate and appreciate both individual and team contributions.

CELEBRATING INDIVIDUALS

Give personal hand-written notes of thanks or congratulations (possibly mailed to his or her home).

Pass along positive comments from others.

Treat to coffee, drink, lunch, etc.

Develop "walls of fame," "alcoves of excellence," or websites filled with pictures, awards, performance/achievement charts, appreciative letters, and success stories.

Reward with greater responsibility, autonomy, and more self-management.

Further align/assign work and/or remove barriers to allow the person to do more of what they do best.

Provide more work that he or she finds especially meaningful or fulfilling.

Invite to a meeting in which he or she wouldn't normally be included.

Provide opportunities for training or personal development.

Sponsor his or her special cause or charity.

Send birthday, Christmas, anniversary, and special-occasion cards to their home.

Respect his or her sensitivities and preferences.

Accommodate personal needs (time off, flex time, special need, etc.).

A small personal gift, uniquely appealing to their hobby or interest.

Gift certificates or tickets (include spouse/family if appropriate).

Send reinforcing articles/books.

Praise him or her to their peers, spouse, or friends.

Send him or her on a special field/site trip.

Ask him or her to develop, train, or support someone else.

Get a very senior manager to give him or her personal thanks/recognition and/or send a personal note.

Send a complimentary email or thank you message to his or her key senior manager and copy him or her.

Get someone to whom they really made a difference to make a special presentation or award.

Remove a barrier or irritant.

Return a report, memo, or email with complimentary margin notes or messages on the quality of their work or importance of their contribution.

Ask for their help/input with a management problem/issue.

Have him or her run the meeting.

Put them in charge of a special project.

Celebrating teams

Cook/serve a special meal to express thanks or congratulations.

Spontaneous treats (e.g. doughnuts, cake, ice cream, pizza) for passing a milestone or to celebrate a win along the way.

Balloons and streamers to accompany giving awards, etc.

Charts or posters showing team progress.

Posting team pictures and their stories/achievements.

Have teams present their accomplishments/projects/progress to executives, visitors, organization meetings, etc.

Have teams featured or make presentations at industry or technical conferences.

Conduct team trips to external partners.

Add to the team's Laughter Index with humorous or fun activities or events.

Make up team plaques, pins, trophies, certificates, hats, mugs, T-shirts, etc.

Have a senior manager drop by a team meeting or work area with special thanks, celebration, or presentation.

Hold special days on which teams can set up a "trade show booth" in lobbies, exhibit halls, hotel ballrooms, to show what they've been doing and connect others to their work.

Give greater responsibility, autonomy, and more self-management.

Help teams enhance or "fun up" their physical workplace environment.

There is a very direct connection between the number of these approaches used and how energized and mobilized people in that leader's organization really are.

Effective communication mobilizes and energizes.

SPEAKING OF SUCCESS

The man who can think but does not know how to express what he thinks is at the same level as he who cannot think.

PERICLES, ATHENIAN STATESMAN, 495-429 B.C.

An old philosophical riddle asks, does a tree falling in the woods make a sound if there's no one there to hear it? The answer depends upon our notion of "sound." If it exists only to the extent that eardrums or other instruments are present to translate sonic energy waves into sound, there is no sound. So we might say that the tree did not make a sound.

We can pose a similar leadership riddle. If no one receives what a manager transmits, does that communication exist? Here, too, the answer depends upon a definition – this time, of the term "communication." If the receiver does not listen to the sender and respond in some way then, as in the example above, there is no communication. There is only noise.

Information vs. communication

"Half the world is composed of people who have something to say and can't, and the other half who have nothing to say and keep saying it."
ROBERT FROST

Many managers are great at supplying information, but they're not so good at communication. This is, after all, the information age. Our organizational lives are overflowing with emails, voice mails, phone calls, newsletters, books, articles, manuals, and web pages. But we suffer from a profound lack of communication. Too many managers over-inform and under-communicate.

The differences between information and communication underscore those between managers and leaders, as shown in the table below.

"[Communication is] based on the same root as communion, which denotes an intense, two-way sharing or exchange – a coming together of thoughts and ideas. Real communication has to do with careful listening, observation, and dialogue..."

FREDERICK REICHHELD, *LOYALTY RULES! HOW TODAY'S LEADERS BUILD LASTING RELATIONSHIPS*

INFORMATION	**COMMUNICATION**
Speaks to the head	Engages the heart
Monologue	Dialog
Facts and Results	Stories and Values
Mostly written	Mostly verbal
Quantity	Quality
Provides updates	Builds communion

Tell me a story

"Leadership is autobiographical. If I don't know your life story, I don't know a thing about you as a leader."

NOEL M. TICHY, PROFESSOR AT THE UNIVERSITY OF MICHIGAN BUSINESS SCHOOL AND PAST DIRECTOR OF GE'S LEADERSHIP DEVELOPMENT CENTER

My decades of speaking and writing about leadership have reinforced that people "get it" most often through a good story, metaphor, or analogy. I know I have connected with an audience when people tell or send me their stories. I enjoy this immensely and have added to my bag of stories along the way. When I had my first leadership job I heard management author and speaker Charles Jones advise, "never make a point without a story and never tell a story without a point." Great advice. I have tried hard to follow it throughout my career.

Philosophies are useful. Strategies chart the way. Frameworks and models outline the tasks ahead. Bullet points provide a checklist. But stories connect. Stories speak to the heart. Stories stir the imagination. Stories rouse our emotions. The most powerful story is one that gets people laughing and then gives them a key point to chew on while their mouths (and minds) are open.

"Leaders have an enormous impact on the overall emotions of an organization, and they are often at the center of the organization's stories. Managing the myths, the legends, and the symbols of the office can be a powerful driver of change. By using the symbolic power of their role to model emotional intelligence, leaders can create new, positive myths through even small gestures and actions."

DANIEL GOLEMAN, RICHARD BYATZIS, AND ANNIE MCKEE, *PRIMAL LEADERSHIP: REALIZING THE POWER OF EMOTIONAL INTELLIGENCE*

"For thousands of years wise leaders have known that the best way to teach lessons about values and principles is through stories. It is still true in today's digital age… The holier-than-thou, finger-wagging moralizer is easy to tune out, whereas as a good storyteller commands rapt attention."

FREDERICK REICHHELD, *LOYALTY RULES! HOW TODAY'S LEADERS BUILD LASTING RELATIONSHIPS*

"We have found that the most effective persuaders use language in a particular way. They supplement numerical data with examples, stories, metaphors, and analogies to make their positions come alive. That use of language paints a vivid word picture and, in doing so, lends a compelling and tangible quality to the persuader's point of view."

JAY CONGER, "THE NECESSARY ART OF PERSUASION"

"The stories people tell about themselves, others, and their activities consciously and subconsciously create meaning and define the way people understand their 'realities.'"

DEBRA MEYERSON, *TEMPERED RADICALS: HOW PEOPLE USE DIFFERENCE TO INSPIRE CHANGE AT WORK*

Powers of persuasion

"The ability to express an idea is well nigh as important as the idea itself."

BERNARD BARUCH, AMERICAN FINANCIER AND GOVERNMENT ADVISER

Bob was clearly frustrated. "I keep telling them, but nobody listens," he fumed. But as we proceeded with the assessment we were doing for Bob's organization, it became apparent that there was a reason nobody was listening to him. The simple truth was that Bob's verbal communication skills were awful. Part of the problem was that Bob believed logical arguments were all he needed to show the wisdom of his proposals. But his analytical approach often created an emotional tone that felt cold and uncaring. Most people felt that Bob didn't care much for them or their point of view because he was focused on providing them with the right answers – which, of course, just happened to be his.

Bob's problem is common among managers who rely heavily on "position power" to get their points across to others. He believed that because he was boss, there was little need to explain or persuade. In "The Necessary Art of Persuasion," published in the *Harvard Business Review*, Jay Conger advises old-school managers like Bob: "If there ever was a time for businesspeople to learn the fine art of persuasion, it is now. Gone are the command-and-control days of executives managing by decree. Today businesses are run largely by cross-functional teams of peers and populated by baby boomers and their Generation X offspring, who show little tolerance for unquestioned authority."

Words are the arsenal of leadership.
WINSTON CHURCHILL

Influencing others is a learned skill. Some people are predisposed to being more charismatic and persuasive. But like emotional intelligence, influence is a learned behavior. We can improve our verbal communication skills through training and development. It's a choice.

Research on communication, influence, and persuasion shows that the most effective influencers – leaders – do much of the following:

- Understand that influencing is as much a process of listening, learning, and negotiating, as it is of convincing and selling. This comes from a core value of looking for the common ground that will produce a win/win outcome.
- See persuasion as more of an ongoing process than an event. The process involves gathering input (what Stephen Covey calls seeking first to understand before trying to be understood), testing a new position, developing a modified approach from that, testing again, and so on.
- Know that everyone is tuned into radio station WIFM (What's in it for Me). Influence-leaders uncover and talk in terms of the other person's interest and how they will win.
- Balance logic and emotion. Persuasion has been described as "logic on fire." Influence-leaders use well-constructed arguments that connect emotionally with their audience through examples, stories, metaphors, or analogies.
- Continually work at improving their verbal communication skills. Informing and managing can be done by email. Communicating and leading takes lots of face-to-face contact. University of Southern California president Stephen Sample declares, "Any leader who thinks that a memo is as effective as a face-to-face meeting, or that an

Effective listening

"One of Warren Bennis' axioms is that a leader should be able to bring out the best in those around him. In making that case, Warren loves to cite an old story about the difference between 19th-century British prime ministers William Gladstone and Benjamin Disraeli. It was said that, when you had dinner with Gladstone, you left feeling that he was the wittiest, most brilliant, most charming person on earth. But when you had dinner with Disraeli, you left feeling that you were the wittiest, most brilliant, most charming person on earth.

In this respect, Bennis and Disraeli are exactly alike. Warren's magnificently fine-tuned "personal radar" makes him extremely sensitive and receptive to what other people are thinking, feeling and saying. I've never encountered a person who is a better listener – who has that rare ability to make you feel as though you were the only person in the world."

STEPHEN B. SAMPLE, "THE ART AND ADVENTURE OF COLLABORATING WITH WARREN BENNIS," *USC TROJAN FAMILY MAGAZINE*

e-mail is as effective as a phone call, is still playing in the minor leagues."

- Adjust their position to incorporate the points of view of those they are trying to get on side. This is listening and learning. It also recognizes that if I don't listen and respond to you, then you'll do the same to me.
- Build alliances, networks, and coalitions for long-term change or improvement. This often means waiting for the right time or the right people to present an opportunity to move the change agenda forward.
- Understand and leverage the dynamics of their organization's culture, such as where power is wielded and who listens to whom.
- Appreciate that credibility is the influence-leader's major currency. We can only write checks on what's in our credibility account. Credibility deposits in our "influence bank accounts" come from keeping commitments, doing our homework, proven expertise, our performance track record, values consistency and congruence, demonstrated respectfulness, and our authenticity.
- Create a solid cause and case for change. Influence-leaders don't make the rookie mistake of jumping straight to the change without taking the audience through the same thinking or planning process he or she went through.
- Use humor to build rapport and connect with people. Studies show that the most effective leaders use humor two to three times more often than their less effective (and more uptight) counterparts.
- Know that generally the bigger the change, the more time it takes. Successful influence-leaders understand that most "overnight successes" take many years.

FROM KNOWING TO DOING

Reflect. Understand. Do.

Leadership is Action

'I wear the chain I forged in life,' replied the Ghost. 'I made it link by link, and yard by yard; I girded it on of my own free will, and of my own free will I wore it.'

CHARLES DICKENS, *A CHRISTMAS CAROL*

Dickens' *A Christmas Carol* is one of the best known and loved stories in the English language. It appeals to people on many levels. One reason I like it so much is because of it provides powerful and timeless leadership development lessons. The principal character, Ebenezer Scrooge, begins his career as a passionate, driven young idealist, only to become a bitter, lonely old man. He's a business and financial success but a failure as a human being. You might say that Scrooge developed a rather large work-life balance problem!

Scrooge's story is one of revelation, reflection, and renewal. It begins one Christmas Eve with a visit from the ghost of his old business partner, Jacob Marley, miserably fettered in long chains and condemned to walk the Earth seeking to do the good he failed to pursue during his life. But as bad as his fate is, he warns, Scrooge's promises to be worse: In the seven years since Marley died, Scrooge had forged an even more "ponderous chain" – but one that he had a chance of casting off if he is visited by the spirits of Christmas past, Christmas present, and Christmas future. While Scrooge is understandably reluctant to welcome them, the spirits ultimately help him to remember his life as it was, see his life as it is now, and preview the bleak future that awaits him if his existing path remains as it is. Awakening Christmas morning, his power to change still intact, Scrooge is a man transformed. He alters the course of his life – and the future to which it leads.

Scrooge's experiences are a good example for any leader to follow. We need to look back to understand what has created the attitudes and behaviors that shape our current circumstances. We need to take a good look around us today to really see what's happening and where we fit into the current picture. Would the young person we once were be proud of what we have become?

Finally, we need to project our current course into the future. If we keep doing what we've been doing, we'll keep getting what we've been getting. Is that good news? Are we on the right track to our preferred future? Or are we continuing to lead in the same old way while expecting different results from our organizations? Of course, that's the path to getting what we've always got. But as I have emphasized throughout this book (and, previously, in *Growing the Distance*), to change them I need to change me.

Ultimately Scrooge's story is one of renewal and hope. By changing his current thinking and behavior, he changes his future – and enriches the lives of others.

There's no short-cut to real leadership.

HANDS ON THE WHEEL

Confidence is that feeling by which the mind embarks on great and honorable courses with a sure hope and trust in itself.

CICERO

Seasoned navigators know that the shortest distance between two points is a straight line. Chasing the wind, veering wildly off in one direction and another, may give the appearance of speed, but actually results in little forward progress.

So it is with leaders. They understand that there's no short-cut to reaching their team's or organization's preferred future. It takes clear vision, a steady hand, and the discipline to avoid quick-fix solutions, however tempting they may be.

The fact is that "quick fix" is an oxymoron. It belongs right up there with dry ice, fuzzy logic, political science, pretty ugly, and rap music (this revealed to me as the parent of three teenagers).

Why crash diets don't work

On average, people in Western cultures put on a half pound per year over much of their adult lives. That comes from an excess intake of just 10 to 20 calories a day. It's about the equivalent of a Ritz cracker a day! For most of us, the formula to keeping our weight under control is pretty simple: eat less and exercise more. But it's so much easier said than done. So we go on crash diets. Research now shows that this lowers our metabolic rate. When we slip off the diet (which is often unsustainable over the long term), the pounds now pile up faster. The BIG challenge – and key to better health – is changing our lifestyle.

There are no leadership formulas. But managers keep searching for them anyway. So they buy the books, hire the consultants, and set up the training programs – whatever happens to offer the latest steps, secrets, or systems that will transform mundane Clark Kent managers into Superman leaders. Most of it is just a waste of time and money.

After three decades of experience with hundreds of management teams, I have found that many of "the latest" management theories amount to little more than a rehash of what has gone before. That's why I find myself in vigorous agreement with MIT's Sloan School of Management professor Edgar Schein when he says, "We go through cycles. Every few years we rediscover formal planning, then we rediscover the importance of people, and then in another few years we discover cost control. When you look over the last forty or fifty years there is nothing much that is genuinely new. It is a recycling and elaboration of something that has been proposed as far back as Plato."

The fact is that meaningful change happens only by applying the timeless leadership principles as I have tried to describe in this book. The results probably won't be instantaneous, but they will last.

The Leader's Progress

"The man who removes a mountain begins by carrying away small stones."

CHINESE PROVERB

As *Growing the Distance* and *The Leader's Digest* have emphasized throughout our discussions around the timeless principles of our Leadership Wheel (page 22), leadership is an inside job. We change them by first changing me. A growing mountain of research, like that on Emotional Intelligence, shows that leadership begins "in here" and moves "out there." That calls for changing our lifestyle. It means developing new habits. Here are a few suggestions:

- Get feedback on how your leadership is perceived by those you are leading. Find out what they think you should keep doing, stop doing, and start doing.
- Set aside a regular time for reflection and renewal (R&R) to stay focused and review the progress of your personal improvement.
- Train, train, train. Take lots of development programs for the skills outlined throughout *The Leader's Digest.*
- Teach those skills to others. Teaching takes us to a much deeper level of understanding and mastery.
- Participate in personal growth retreats or workshops that help you focus on the inner dimension of leadership.

The Ant and the Grasshopper

In a field one summer's day a Grasshopper was hopping about, chirping and singing to its heart's content. An Ant passed by, bearing along with great toil an ear of corn he was taking to the nest.

"Why not come and chat with me," said the Grasshopper, "instead of toiling and moiling in that way?"

"I am helping to lay up food for the winter," said the Ant, and recommend you to do the same."

"Why bother about winter?" said the Grasshopper; "we have got plenty of food at present." But the Ant went on its way and continued its toil. When the winter came the grasshopper had no food and found itself dying of hunger, while it saw the ants distributing every day corn and grain from the stores they had collected in the summer. Then the Grasshopper knew:

Don't wait until necessity is upon you. Be prepared by taking action now.

AESOP

- Complete self-assessment tests that help you understand your leadership style and how you relate with other styles – especially those most opposite to your own.
- Monitor your job happiness. What turns you on? What turns you off? What are your greatest strengths? How much of your job plays to your strengths? Are you in the right job?
- Find a mentor who can give you the benefit of his or her experience.
- Hire a coach to assess your team's effectiveness and review your leadership. Work with him or her to address key issues and make personal and/or team improvements.

Understanding the timeless leadership principles is easy. Our challenge is to apply them.

Practiced Excellence

Great things are not done by impulse but by a series of small things brought together.

Vincent Van Gogh

Years ago my previous consulting company, The Achieve Group, worked with Zenger Miller and Tom Peters delivering a cultural leadership development program entitled, "Toward Excellence." It helped management teams act on the leadership principles outlined in Peters' and Waterman's international mega-bestseller, *In Search of Excellence*. As the book climbed the bestseller charts, many people (especially jealous colleagues) dismissed it as "a blinding flash of the obvious."

Guilty as charged. There was nothing new in that excellence research. But the big problem wasn't with understanding excellence. The problem was with living it. Knowing isn't doing. Common sense is so seldom common practice. So we entitled the introductory module of our development program, "Obviously the Obvious Isn't So Obvious."

Seek out the new

After dinner at a Chinese restaurant, our family compared the contents of their fortune cookies. One of the cookies read "no one who has reached the age of wisdom can be told what to do." I commented that this was a good observation about the power of choice – no one can tell us what to do if we see life as a series of choices. To which our son, Chris, piped up, "or it means you are a stubborn old geezer."

We need to guard against becoming stubborn old geezers. Highly effective leaders are constantly seeking out and digesting new perspectives and experiences to keep them fresh and alive. They are continually looking for ways to grow themselves and those they lead.

There is really nothing new in *The Leader's Digest*. These timeless principles have been around for thousands of years. They have guided us through the good times and the bad, stretching back through the mists of time. Because our forebears lived by many of these principles, life has steadily progressed from the Stone Age through the rise of many civilizations and incredible human achievements. Because of the relentless application of these leadership principles, today we enjoy a lifestyle unimaginable not too many centuries – or even decades – ago. The timeless leadership principles will be rediscovered and renamed many more times in the centuries ahead. And they'll lead the generations to follow us to places we can't imagine today.

I hope the *The Leader's Digest* has helped light your personal development path for the short time that we've traveled together. I hope you refer to it often for its many digestible nuggets of inspiration and ideas. If you would like further leadership inspiration or ideas, please visit our large and growing website at www.clemmer.net. I would love to hear your feedback on *The Leader's Digest* (or any of my other books). Please email me personally at jim.clemmer@clemmer.net.

Finally, remember that leadership is an action, not a position. May it be that I have helped you in some way to act like a leader. And may our leadership paths cross again soon.

Appendix A

Growing the Distance

Timeless principles for personal, career and family success

> *"Growing the Distance is a road map of the heart that vividly describes the personal development pathways and towns along the way and lets you choose which ones to stop at. I really enjoyed the book's multi-level layout and flowing writing style."*

Growing the Distance was written for anyone, regardless of his or her role or position, who wants to be a more effective leader. I have been very gratified by the wide variety of people who continue to send me emails or tell me about what a difference the book made in their lives. High school classes have studied *Growing the Distance* and emailed me reports on how they've applied the principles. Colleges and universities have used *Growing the Distance* in leadership development programs and had me speak to groups of their students.

People who have gone through great traumas – such as the loss of loved ones or serious illnesses and accidents – have benefited from this book. (One reader sent me a detailed email about how *Growing the Distance* helped her long hospitalization and recovery after she was hit by a lightening bolt that killed someone else in her group at a picnic.) Hundreds of organizations have purchased *Growing the Distance* to give to all their employees for their personal development and to build a more "leaderful" organization. (See page 206 for information on quantity discounts.) Many teams and departments have started study or discussion groups to talk about applying the timeless principles in their personal and professional lives.

Every word of *Growing the Distance* has been excerpted and indexed into short, column-sized articles, which are available on our website (www.clemmer.net), and are generating tens of thousands of "hits" per month. Many of these excerpts have been reproduced in newsletters, magazines, websites, and electronic publications around the world. The CLEMMER Group's complementary Improvement Points email subscription service sends out short quotes from *Growing the Distance* and my other books and columns (as well as links to original sources) to thousands of subscribers several times a week.

Take advantage of substantial discounts when you purchase multiple copies of *The Leader's Digest* and *Growing the Distance*

VALUABLE RESOURCES FOR EVERYONE IN YOUR ORGANIZATION

For professional and personal development, *The Leader's Digest* and *Growing the Distance* are ideal complements. Each book (or both) is suitable for distribution in quantity by executives, managers, and training professionals attempting to help people throughout their organizations:

- embrace personal growth and development as a key to dealing with continuous and unpredictable change
- provide a strong base for leadership development programs
- build a common foundation of values around its timeless principles
- establish a broader "context of being" for training programs teaching technical, process, or behavioral "skills of doing"
- bring teams together with a common language and set of values
- help everyone in the organization become leaders
- nurture ongoing personal growth and development

***The Leaders Digest* and *Growing the Distance* also make great gifts for:**

- young people getting started in life
- someone contemplating career changes and choices
- people wrestling with major change or a crisis
- someone who's lost their job or had it dramatically changed
- people feeling unfocused and listless
- managers, entrepreneurs, and executives looking to increase their leadership effectiveness
- people "on the grow" always looking for personal development
- customers, suppliers, distributors, dealers, and other partners

Major discounts are available for multiple copies of *The Leader's Digest* and *Growing the Distance*. Visit The CLEMMER Group's website (www.clemmer.net) or call toll-free 1-888-925-GROW (4769) for more information.

Website Resources on Practical Leadership

Visit our rich and ever-expanding Organization Transformation, Leadership Development, and Personal Effectiveness resource center on-line!

www.clemmer.net

- **Free articles and columns**. Browse through over 250 timely articles by topic, covering personal, team, and organization development.
- **Looking for inspiration? Words of wisdom?** Sign up for our complimentary *Improvement Points* service – powerful quotes with links to full articles, delivered to you by e-mail three times a week.
- **Booking Jim Clemmer.** Extensive information on Jim's practical leadership approaches, background and experience, keynote presentations, workshops, and management team retreats.
- **Jim Clemmer's free e-Newsletter.** Subscribe to Jim Clemmer's *Leader Letter* for how-to tips and techniques, current insights, leadership debates, and discussions.
- **Key models and frameworks**. It all starts here! Check out the core frameworks that inspire action and achieve results. Jim evolved these practical applications over years of extensive research, writing, and application.
- **Complimentary on-line assessments and presentations**. Organizational and personal assessments and insights.
- **Books, CDs, and tapes**. Check out sample chapters, excerpts, reviews, and more! Help develop "leaders on the grow" by sharing these practical resources with team members (or family and friends)! Deep discounts (between 45 and 76% off list price) start at just 10 books.
- ***Growing the Distance On-Line***. Our powerful personal growth and leadership development workshop.
- **Recommended reading**. Browse through hundreds of books organized by topic area, all recommended to help you blaze your pathways to ever higher performance.
- **Site seeing**. Links to recommended websites for organizational and personal improvement.
- **Information** on The CLEMMER Group's coaching and consulting services.

JIM CLEMMER, CSP

Practical Leadership: Inspiring *Action*, Achieving Results

CUT THROUGH THE LEADERSHIP THEORIES, GENERALITIES, AND CLICHÉS

Let's Get Practical!

- **Get practical inspiration at your next meeting.** Hire Jim to customize a high-energy keynote presentation tailored to your group.
- **Get practical leadership and organization development.** Exploit Jim's expertise in change, customer service, and high performance culture.
- **Get practical management team development.** Use Jim to boost leadership team effectiveness and propel the organization forward.
- **Get practical resources that inspire *action* and achieve results.** Buy Jim's popular how-to books, CDs, tapes, and subscription services.
- **Get practical coaching and consulting.** Achieve breakthrough results with Jim and his team of experts.

Books, Keynotes, Workshop/Retreats, Management Team Development, and Consulting

For over 25 years Jim Clemmer's practical leadership approaches have been inspiring action and achieving results. His over 2,000 presentations and workshops/retreats, five bestselling books, columns, and newsletters are helping hundreds of thousands of managers worldwide because they are inspiring, instructive, and refreshingly fun. And best of all... *they work!* He distills his exhaustive research, extensive experience, and collection of best practices into easily understood, highly energizing, and practical applications.

Visit www.clemmer.net for details or call (519) 748-6561

The CLEMMER Group Inc.
10 Pioneer Drive, Suite 105
Kitchener, ON N2P 2A4
Phone: (519) 748-1044
Fax: (519) 748-5813
E-mail: service@clemmer.net

NOTES

Chapter 1: Leaders Make the Difference

Page 13: "There's no avoiding it..." Geoffrey Colvin, "The Changing Art of Becoming Unbeatable," *FORTUNE,* Nov. 24, 1997, p. 300, © 1997 – Time Inc. All rights reserved.

Page 14: [sidebar] "One hospital had significantly better results..." Lance Secretan, *Inspirational Leadership* (Toronto: Macmillan Canada, 1999), p. 131.

Page 16: "A Wharton [School of the University of Pennsylvania] study found..." Geoffrey Colvin, "The Changing Art of Becoming Unbeatable," *FORTUNE,* Nov. 24, 1997, p. 300, © 1997 – Time Inc. All rights reserved.

"In the most admired companies..." *FORTUNE,* Oct. 26, 1998, p. 218, © 1998 – Time Inc. All rights reserved.

Page 17: "Leadership and management are two distinctive..." John Kotter, "What Leaders Really Do," *Harvard Business Review,* vol. 79, no. 11, © 2001 by The Harvard Business School Publishing Corporation; all rights reserved.

Page 20: [sidebar] "Management is getting people..." Warren Bennis, "A Guide to Understanding the Many Different Dimensions of Leadership," Toolpack Consulting, http://users.utu.fi/juhtiur/jakelu/leader.pdf

Page 25: [sidebar] "Leaders have always played a primordial..." Daniel Goleman, Richard Boyatzis and Annie McKee, *Primal Leadership: Realizing the Power of Emotional Intelligence* (Boston, MA: Harvard Business School Press, 2002), p. 5. Reprinted by permission of Harvard Business School Press. Copyright © 2002 by Daniel Goleman, all rights reserved.

Page 26: "There now is a considerable body of research ..." Cary Cherniss, "Emotional Intelligence: What it is and why it Matters," posted on the website for the Consortium for Research on Emotional Intelligence in Organizations (www.eiconsortium.org).

"We know that emotional intelligence can be enhanced..." Steven Stein and Howard Book, *The EQ Edge: Emotional Intelligence and Your Future* (Toronto: Stoddart, 2000), pp. 23-24.

Page 28: "Competency research in over 200 companies ..." Cary Cherniss, "The Business Case for Emotional Intelligence," posted on the website for the Consortium for Research on Emotional Intelligence in Organizations (www.eiconsortium.org).

"Over the past five years, MHS..." Steven Stein and Howard Book, *The EQ Edge: Emotional Intelligence and Your Future,* p. 4.

Chapter 2: Focus and Context

Page 29: "Successful leaders spend a lot of time..." Interview with John Alexander, president of the Center For Creative Leadership, from the Center's e-Newsletter, Oct. 2001.

Page 30: [sidebar] "Maintaining focus is a key to success..." Bill Gates, "Virtual Bill," *Profit,* Oct.-Nov. 1997, p. 79.

[sidebar] "I've learned that only through focus..." Brent Schlender, "Bill Gates @ Work," *FORTUNE,* July 8, 2002, © 2002 – Time Inc. All rights reserved.

Page 31: [sidebar] "The primary task of leadership is to communicate the vision..." Frederick Smith, "All in a Day's Work," *Harvard Business Review,* vol. 79, no. 11, © 2001 by The Harvard Business School Publishing Corporation; all rights reserved.

Page 32: "Leadership is about coping with change..." John Kotter, "What Leaders Really Do," *Harvard Business Review,* vol. 79, no. 11, © 2001 by The Harvard Business School Publishing Corporation; all rights reserved.

Page 33: [sidebar] "We are forever looking for a cure..." David Whyte, *The Heart Aroused: Poetry and Preservation of the Soul in Corporate America* (New York: Doubleday, 1994), pp. 280-281.

Page 37: [sidebar] "It came in the heat of a discussion..." *Executive Success: Making It in Management,* Eliza G. C. Collins, ed., (New York: Wiley, 1983), p. 199.

Page 38: [sidebar] "Of these sixteen types of forecasts..." William A. Sherden, *The Fortune Sellers: The Big Business of Buying and Selling Predictions* (New York: John Wiley & Sons, 1998), p. iii. Copyright © 2000. This material is used by permission of John Wiley & Sons Inc.

[sidebar] "Even with all the advances in science..." William A. Sherden, *The Fortune Sellers: The Big Business of Buying and Selling Predictions,* p. 6. Copyright © 2000. This material is used by permission of John Wiley & Sons Inc.

Page 40: "Vision is one of the least understood..." from "Aligning Action and Values," The Forum, June 2000, posted at www.jimcollins.com.

Page 42: "Leaders need to energize people..." Cynthia Tragge-Lakra, "All in a Day's Work," *Harvard Business Review,* vol. 79, no. 11, © 2001 by The Harvard Business School Publishing Corporation; all rights reserved.

Page 43: "Oh, the place you'll go..." Dr.Seuss, *Seuss-isms for Success* (New York: Random House, 1999).

Page 45: "Values are the bedrock..." TERRENCE DEAL AND ALLAN KENNEDY, *CORPORATE CULTURES: THE RITES AND RITUALS OF CORPORATE LIFE* (Reading, MA: Addison-Wesley, 1982), p. 21.

Page 48: "Worthwhile work..." Mark Albion, *Making a Life, Making a Living* (New York: Warner Books, 2000), pp. 91-92.

Page 49 "A Boston College study..." Charles Garfield, *Peak Performers* (New York: Morrow, 1986). p. 103.

"The Vermont-based Center..." Tad Tulega, *Beyond the Bottom Line* (Briston,VT: Soundview Executive Book Summaries, 1985), p. 3.

"Consultant and former Harvard professor..." Interview by David Creelman, June 4, 2001, posted at www.hr.com.

Page 50: "Companies that spend money to develop..." from "Bottom line linked to ethics: report," *The Globe & Mail,* Aug. 14, 2001, page B8.

Page 51 "An organization without human commitment..." Henry Mintzberg, "Managing Government, Governing Management," *Harvard Business Review,* vol. 74, no. 3, © 1996 by The Harvard Business School Publishing Corporation; all rights reserved.

Page 52 "In his book, *The Hungry Spirit:...*" Charles Handy, *The Hungry Spirit: Beyond Capitalism – A Quest for Purpose in the Modern World* (London: Hutchinson, 1997), p. 77.

"Writing in *Fortune* magazine..." Geoffrey Colvin, "Should Companies Care?," *FORTUNE,* June 11, 2001, p. 60, © 2001 – Time Inc. All rights reserved.

Chapter 3: Responsibility for Choices

Page 57: "Whenever we seek to avoid..." Scott Peck, *The Road Less Traveled* (New York: Simon & Schuster, 1978), p. 42.

Page 60 "No one wants to work for a grouch..." Daniel Goleman, Richard Boyatzis and Annie McKee, *Primal Leadership: Realizing the Power of Emotional Intelligence* (Boston, MA: Harvard Business School Press, 2002), pp. 12 and 14. Reprinted by permission of Harvard Business School Press. Copyright © 2002 by Daniel Goleman, all rights reserved.

Page 61 "A University of Michigan study of 70 work teams..." Daniel Goleman, Richard Boyatzis and Annie McKee, *Primal Leadership: Realizing the Power of Emotional Intelligence* (Boston: Harvard Business School Press, 2002), p. 46. Reprinted by permission of Harvard Business School Press. Copyright © 2002 by Daniel Goleman, all rights reserved.

"Learned helplessness is the giving-up reaction..." Martin Seligman, *Learned Optimism* (New York: Knopf, 1990), pp. 15-16.

Page 63 "Everything can be taken from a man..." Viktor Frankl, *Man's Search for Meaning: Experiences in the Concentration Camp* (New York: Washington Square Press, 1985), pp. 86-87.

Page 64 "I firmly believe that most barriers are self-imposed..." W Mitchell, *It's Not What Happens to You, It's What You Do About It* (Arvada: Phoenix Press, 1999), pp. 94-95.

Page 65 "Nothing, absolutely nothing is absolute..." W Mitchell, *It's Not What Happens to You, It's What You Do About It* (Arvada: Phoenix Press, 1999), p. xi.

"Many experiments are done with monkeys..." Luke De Sadeleer and Joseph Sherren, *Vitamin C for a Healthy Workplace* (Carp, ON: Creative Bound, 2001), pp. 34-36.

Page 70 "A better way to change a system..." A conversation with Robert Redford, "Turning an Industry Inside Out," *Harvard Business Review*, vol. 80, no. 5, © 2002 by The Harvard Business School Publishing Corporation; all rights reserved.

Page 72 "Research indicates that effective middle leaders..." Quy Nguyen Huy, "In Praise of Middle Managers," *Harvard Business Review*, vol. 79, no. 8, © 2001 by The Harvard Business School Publishing Corporation; all rights reserved.

Page 73 "At one point, I had an extraordinarily difficult boss..." from "Link & Learn Leadership Toolkit," Jan. 23, 2001, www.Linkage-inc.com.

Page 77 "...familiar and disempowering words..." Geoffrey Bellman, *Getting Things Done When You're Not in Charge* (San Francisco: Berrett-Koehler, 2001), pp. 93-94.

"...leaders must understand that leadership is not just a job..." from an interview with John Kotter in the LeadershipToolkit (LeadershipToolkit@EMKTG.Linkage-inc.com), Jan. 23, 2001.

Page 78 "Tempered radicals lead through inspiration..." Debra Meyerson, *Tempered Radicals: How People Use Difference to Inspire Change at Work* (Boston, MA: Harvard Business School Press, 2001), pp. 170, xi, 5, 7, 176, and 171.

Chapter 4: Authenticity

Page 79: "In the end, it's the quality and character..." Frances Hesselbein, "All in a Day's Work," *Harvard Business Review*, vol. 79, no. 11, © 2001 by The Harvard Business School Publishing Corporation; all rights reserved.

Page 80 [sidebar] "Leaders need to be aware of the way they present themselves..." John Sasik, "Self-Other Agreement on Charismatic Leadership: Relationships with Work Attitudes and Managerial Performance," *Training*, Feb. 2002, p. 25.

"The first piece of advice we give to people..." Cynthia Tragge-Lakra, "All in a Day's Work," *Harvard Business Review*, vol. 79, no. 11, © 2001 by The Harvard Business School Publishing Corporation; all rights reserved.

Page 84 "The boy rode on the donkey..." Mark Albion , from his newsletter ML2 E-News #92 – "Where Are You Trying to Get," Jan. 23, 2002 (www.makingalife.com).

Page 86 "A survey by The Discovery Group..." from www.discoverysurveys.com.

"For example, a Lakewood Research study asked..." Patrick L. Townsend & Joan Gebhardt, *Recognition, Gratitude & Celebration* (Menlo Park, CA: Crisp Publications, 1997), p. 19.

Page 87 "A study of the eight biggest automobile manufacturers..." John T. Landry, "The Value of Trust," *Harvard Business Review*, vol. 76, no. 1, © 1998 by The Harvard Business School Publishing Corporation; all rights reserved.

"A study commissioned by *Macleans* magazine..." from "The Top 100 Employers," *Macleans*, Oct. 28, 2002.

Page 90 [sidebar] "...respect is at the top of the list..." Virginia Galt, "Bosses Don't Know Employees: Seminar," *The Globe & Mail*, Dec. 27, 2001.

[sidebar] "Most labor disputes are not really about money..." Jody Hoffer Gittell, "Investing in Relationships," *Harvard Business Review*, vol. 79, no. 6, © 2001 by The Harvard Business School Publishing Corporation; all rights reserved.

Page 92 "Alexander the Great was leading his forces..." Arthur F. Lenehan, *The Best of Bits & Pieces,* (Fairfield, NJ: The Economics Press, 1994), p. 108.

Page 97 "In a longitudinal study of the effectiveness of leaders. . ." Daniel Goleman, Richard Boyatzis and Annie McKee, *Primal Leadership: Realizing the Power of Emotional Intelligence* (Boston: Harvard Business School Press, 2002), p. 136. Reprinted by permission of Harvard Business School Press. Copyright © 2002 by Daniel Goleman, all rights reserved.

Page 103 [sidebar] "During World War II, Winston Churchill..." from "Why Companies Fail," *FORTUNE,* May 27, 2002, p. 56, © 2002 – Time Inc. All rights reserved.

Chapter 5: Passion and Commitment

Page 106: "The Gallup organization found that only 29%..." from "Driving Performance in the Emotional Economy: A GMJ Q&A with Curt W. Coffman," *Gallup Management Journal,* Jan. 9, 2003, posted at http:gmj.gallup.com.

"A Towers Perrin survey showed that 13% of employees..." Virginia Galt, "Are Workers Loyal? Not Likely," *The Globe & Mail,* Aug. 31, 2001.

"More than 90% of people surveyed in a *Psychology Today* study..." Luke De Sadeleer and Joseph Sherren, *Vitamin C for a Healthy Workplace* (Carp, ON: Creative Bound, 2001), pp. 80-81.

Page 107: [sidebar] "Making jobs more rewarding is the best way to influence..." William Denney, from HR.com's ebulletin for week of Mar. 19, 2001.

Page 108: "Our passion for productivity..." Michael Schrage, "I Wasn't Fired," *FORTUNE,* Jan. 21, 2002, p. 128, © 2002 – Time Inc. All rights reserved.

"Great leaders move us..." Daniel Goleman, Richard Boyatzis and Annie McKee, *Primal Leadership: Realizing the Power of Emotional Intelligence* (Boston: Harvard Business School Press, 2002), p. 3. Reprinted by permission of Harvard Business School Press. Copyright © 2002 by Daniel Goleman, all rights reserved.

Page 109 [sidebar] "If management wants employees to take more responsibility..." Chris Argyris, "Empowerment: The Emperor's New Clothes," *Harvard Business Review,* vol. 76, no. 3, © 1998 by The Harvard Business School Publishing Corporation; all rights reserved.

Page 110 "We found that there was a cause-and-effect relationship..." Frederick F. Reichheld, *The Loyalty Effect* (Boston: HBS Press, 1996), p. 2.

"...building loyalty has in fact become the acid test..." Frederick F. Reichheld, *Loyalty Rules!* (Boston: HBS Press, 2001), p. 2.

Page 111 [sidebar] "The University of Michigan Business..." Bronwyn Fryer, "The Science of Satisfaction," within "High Tech the Old-Fashioned Way," *Harvard Business Review,* vol. 79, no. 3, © 2001 by The Harvard Business School Publishing Corporation; all rights reserved.

[sidebar] "Scott Cook, founder of Intuit..." J. William Gurley, "Web Ads: Why Impressions Don't Matter," *FORTUNE,* July 24, 2000, p. 340, © 2000 – Time Inc. All rights reserved.

"...the bulldog's appearance hasn't improved..." Nick Morgan, "How to Overcome 'Change Fatigue,'" *Harvard Management Update,* July 2001, © 2001 by The Harvard Business School Publishing Corporation; all rights reserved.

Page 112 [sidebar] "The best predictor of customer satisfaction..." from www.customersat.com, Dec. 2000.

[sidebar] "For every one percent increase in internal service..." Daniel Goleman, Richard Boyatzis and Annie McKee, *Primal Leadership: Realizing the Power of Emotional Intelligence* (Boston, MA: Harvard Business School Press, 2002), p. 15. Reprinted by permission of Harvard Business School Press. Copyright © 2002 by Daniel Goleman, all rights reserved.

[sidebar] "In cardiac care units where nurses' moods were depressed..." Daniel Goleman, Richard Boyatzis and Annie McKee, *Primal Leadership: Realizing the Power of Emotional Intelligence* (Boston, MA: Harvard Business School Press, 2002), p. 16. Reprinted by permission of Harvard Business School Press. Copyright © 2002 by Daniel Goleman, all rights reserved.

Page 112: [sidebar] "Cornell's School of Hotel Administration found..." Paul Hemp, "My Week as a Room-Service Waiter at the Ritz," *Harvard Business Review*, vol. 80, no. 6, © 2002 by The Harvard Business School Publishing Corporation; all rights reserved.

[sidebar] "A study of call centers found that "satisfied contact center employees..." from "Study Links CSR Satisfaction And Customer Satisfaction," posted on www.commweb.com, Mar. 1, 2002.

Page 113: "Organizations should be built and managers should be functioning..." from interview an with Henry Mintzberg in "Turning Business Upside Down," *The Costco Connection*, May/June 2002, p. 25.

Page 116: [sidebar] "Building passion and commitment the Wal-Mart way" from "Sam's Rules for Building a Business" at www.walmartstores.com.

Page 117: "A study by J. Howard & Associates..." from "Research Shows Link Between Empowerment and Performance," posted at www.hr.com.

"...you can make a killing by making nice..." Nashua Watson, "Happy Companies Make Happy Investments," *FORTUNE*, May 27, 2002, p. 162, © 2002 – Time Inc. All rights reserved.

"Companies that adopt employee involvement..." from a report by the USC School of Business, posted at www.marshall.usc.edu.

"A study of franchise systems found..." John Southerst, "Recruits Wanted: Entrepreneurs Need not Apply," *The Globe & Mail*, July 9, 1999.

Page 118: "A study by Success Profiles analyzed..." from "Increasing Revenue Growth Through Giving Employees Authority to Make Decisions," posted at www.successprofiles.com.

[sidebar] "Companies with the lowest lost-time injury rates..." from "Corporate Culture: The Key to Safety Performance," *Occupational Hazards*, April, 2000, © 2000 by Penton Media Inc.

Page 120: "Success Profiles studied 150 companies..." from "Feedback & Engagement as a Best Practice," Part II, posted at www.successprofiles.com.

"They also studied organizational communication..." from "Reducing Employee Turnover by Improving Communication," posted at www.successprofiles.com.

Page 121 "A trucking company found..." Frederick Reichheld, *The Loyalty Effect* (Boston: Bain & Company, 1996), p. 96.

"One study estimated it costs a typical..." from "Costly Turnovers," *The Globe & Mail*, Oct. 10, 2000.

Page 122 [sidebar] "Creating commitment cultures" from "Talent Remains in the Spotlight," posted at www.keepem.com. Reprinted with permission of the publisher. From "Love 'Em or Lose 'Em," copyright © 2002 by Beverly L. Kaye, Sharon Jordan-Evans, Berret-Koehler Publishers Inc., San Francisco, CA. All rights reserved. www.bkconnection.com

Page 123 "A study of 200 high-potential leaders..." from "Technology and Feedback: Key Ingredients for Effective Leadership," *Link & Learn* newsletter (Lexington, MA: Linkage Incorporated), March 2001, posted at www.linkageinc.com.

"A WorkLife Design survey reviewed..." Richard Deems, "Good People Stay When. . .," May 8, 2001, posted at www.hr.com.

"Ipsos-Reid asked employees what makes them stay..." Virginia Galt, "Office Work Encroaching on Home Life, Poll Reveals," *The Globe & Mail*, Mar. 27, 2001, p. B9.

Page 124: "So, how do we build loyalty..." Curt W. Coffman, "People Aren't Your Greatest Asset," *Gallup Management Journal*, Feb. 4, 2000, posted at http:gmj.gallup.com.

"Based on a study of over 1 million employees in 330 organizations..." Natalie Southworth, "Managers Crucial to Curbing Turnover," *The Globe & Mail*, May 30, 2001.

Page 127: "A study by the Center for Creative Leadership found..." from David Creelman interview with Helen Handfield-Jones, co-author of *The War for Talent*, in HR.com's eBulletin, Feb. 11, 2002.

Chapter 6: Spirit and Meaning

Page 129: "The search for meaning..." William J. Bennett, *The Moral Compass: Stories for a Life's Journey* (New York: Simon & Schuster, 1995), p. 699.

Page 131: "Listening to the car radio one morning..." Thanks to Mark Henderson for relating the story of the Human Cannonball, which he heard on his car radio.

Page 132 "It's like we have learned to build..." Ian Percy, *Going Deep: Exploring Spirituality in Life and Leadership* (Toronto: Macmillan Canada, 1997), p. 63.

Page 134 "When I hear managers say they're going to be tough..." from an interview with David Creelman, HR.com's ebulletin, June 4, 2001.

"Reflecting on his findings, Mitroff reports..." from an interview with David Creelman, posted at HR.com.

"One poll found that managers want a deeper sense of meaning..." from "Religion in the Workplace," *Businessweek* Online, Nov. 1, 1999.

"Former Harvard professor David Maister's study..." from an interview with David Creelman, HR.com's eBulletin, June 4, 2001.

Page 135 "There is an awakening happening all over..." Ian Percy, *Going Deep: Exploring Spirituality in Life and Leadership* (Toronto: Macmillan Canada, 1997), pp. 85, 88.

Page 137 "This dynamic of meaning making is..." Diane Coutu, "How Resilience Works," *Harvard Business Review*, vol. 80, no. 5, © 2002 by The Harvard Business School Publishing Corporation; all rights reserved.

Page 139 "Barrett outlines the big leadership challenge..." Richard Barrett, "Organizational Transformation: Liberating the Corporate Soul," *Business Spirit Journal Online*, posted at www.bizspirit.com.

Page 143 "Now we have results from a range of industries..." Daniel Goleman, Richard Boyatzis and Annie McKee, *Primal Leadership: Realizing the Power of Emotional Intelligence* (Boston: Harvard Business School Press, 2002), p. 17. Reprinted by permission of Harvard Business School Press. Copyright © 2002 by Daniel Goleman, all rights reserved.

"Southwest Airlines founder Herb Kelleher said..." Eric Schurenberg, "The Fly Boys: Giants of the 20th Century," *FORTUNE*, May 24, 1999, p. 244, © 1999 – Time Inc. All rights reserved.

[sidebar] "Success Profiles studied over 600 businesses..." from "Increasing Profits Through Mission, Vision, and Guiding Principles," posted at www.successprofiles.com.

Page 147 "Right now, your organization has exactly the kind of communication it deserves..." Ian Percy, *Going Deep: Exploring Spirituality in Life and Leadership* (Toronto: Macmillan Canada, 1997), p. 135.

Chapter 7: Growing and Developing

Page 149: "A true Master is not the one..." Neale Donald Walsch, *Conversations With God: An Uncommon Dialogue, Book 1* (New York: Putnam, 1995), p. 114.

Page 150: "We should not confuse human beings with human capital..." Thomas Stewart, "A New Way to Think about Employees," *FORTUNE*, April 13, 1998, p. 169, © 1998 – Time Inc. All rights reserved.

Page 154 "From my research I'm left with the impression..." from "Dr. Boyatzis on Developing Managers," interview with David Creelman, HR.com's ebulletin, May 7, 2001.

Page 156 [sidebar] "I used to be the Public Relations Coordinator..." posted at www.busreslab.com.

Page 159 [sidebar] "...what we expect, all too often..." Robert Tauber, *Self-Fulfilling Prophecy* (Westport, CT: Praeger Publishers, 1997).

Page 161: "The truly engaged and talented people..." Curt W. Coffman, "People Aren't Your Greatest Asset," *Gallup Management Journal*, Feb. 4, 2000, posted at http:gmj.gallup.com.

"...a common ingredient: remediability..." John Thackray, "Feedback for Real," *Gallup Management Journal*, Mar. 15, 2001, posted at http:gmj.gallup.com.

Page 162: "...it is the bosses themselves..." Jean-Francois Manzoni and Jean-Louis Barsoux, "The Set-Up-To-Fail Syndrome," *Harvard Business Review*, vol. 76, no. 2, © 1998 by The Harvard Business School Publishing Corporation; all rights reserved.

Page 163: "The test of a good manager is to make ordinary people..." Luke De Sadeleer and Joseph Sherren, *Vitamin C for a Healthy Workplace* (Carp, ON: Creative Bound, 2001), p. 114.

"...develop their natural talents to such an extent..." Marcus Buckingham, "Don't Waste Time and Money," *Gallup Management Journal,* Dec. 3, 2001, posted at http:gmj.gallup.com.

Page 164: [sidebar] "Keeping poor performers means that development opportunities..." Geoffrey Colvin, "Make Sure You Chop the Dead Wood," *FORTUNE,* Jan. 22, 2001, p. 48, © 2001 – Time Inc. All rights reserved.

[sidebar] "I feel there is no greater disrespect..." Geoffrey Colvin, "Make Sure You Chop the Dead Wood," *FORTUNE,* Jan. 22, 2001, p. 48, © 2001 – Time Inc. All rights reserved.

[sidebar] "Easing someone's path does not mean..." William Bennett, *The Moral Compass* (New York: Simon & Schuster, 1995), p. 364.

Page 165: "If a would-be leader wants glamour..." Steven B. Sample, *The Contrarian's Guide to Leadership* (San Francisco: Jossey-Bass, 2002), p. 122. Copyright © 2002 by Steven B. Sample. This material is used by permission of John Wiley & Sons Inc.

Page 166: "...useful tips for giving good feedback..." Luke De Sadeleer and Joseph Sherren, *Vitamin C for a Healthy Workplace* (Carp, ON: Creative Bound, 2001), pp. 104-105.

Page 167: "Empathic (from empathy) listening gets inside..." Stephen Covey, *The Seven Habits of Highly Effective People* (New York: Simon & Schuster, 1989), pp. 240-241.

Page 169: "Year after year we ask employees what motivates them..." Alfie Kohn, "Rethinking Rewards," *Harvard Business Review,* © 1993 by The Harvard Business School Publishing Corporation; all rights reserved.

Page 170: "All leadership is appreciative leadership..." from an interview with David Creelman, HR.com's ebulletin, July 9, 2001.

[sidebar] "One study of U.S. business school graduates..." from "MBAs Scorn Mom," *The Globe & Mail,* May 28, 1998.

[sidebar] "In a survey of 13,000 managers..." Walter Kiechel, "What Lies Beneath," *Harvard Management Update,* July 2001, © 2001 by The Harvard Business School Publishing Corporation; all rights reserved.

Page 171: "Fully 90% of managers squander their time..." Heike Bruch and Sumantra Ghoshal, "Beware the Busy Manager," *Harvard Business Review,* vol. 80, no. 2, © 2002 by The Harvard Business School Publishing Corporation; all rights reserved.

Chapter 8: Mobilizing and Energizing

Page 173: "Drawing energy out of people..." from "Link & Learn Leadership Toolkit," Jan. 23, 2001, posted at www.linkage-inc.com.

Page 176: "People do work for money..." Jeffrey Pfeffer, "Six Dangerous Myths About Pay," *Harvard Business Review,* vol. 76, no. 3, © 1998 by The Harvard Business School Publishing Corporation; all rights reserved.

Page 177: [sidebar] "The programmers' top three were..." John R. Throop, "Mastering the ABCs of Organizations," posted at www.HR.com, May 1, 2001.

Page 178: "People are not 'things' to be manipulated..." from "The Art of Chaordic Leadership," *Leader to Leader* 15, (Winter 2000), pp. 20-26.

[sidebar] "As soon as I fulfill that expectation..." from "An Interview with James Autry in Des Moines, Iowa," posted at www.greenleaf.org (Greenleaf Center for Creative Leadership).

"...the number of people who are familiar with the servant..." Larry C. Spears, "Servant-Leadership: Quest for Caring Leadership," posted at www.greenleaf.org.

Page 179: [sidebar] "Many are still locked into this idea that an organization is accurately reflected..." from interview with Henry Mintzberg in "Turning Business Upside Down," *The Costco Connection,* May/June 2002, p. 25.

Page 181: "When I was a kid..." Jack Welch, "Personal Histories: Leaders Remember The Moments And People That Shaped Them," *Harvard Business Review,* vol. 79, no. 11, © 2001 The Harvard Business School Publishing Corporation; all rights reserved.

"One study by the Employment Policy Foundation..." Glenn Burkins, "Work Week," *Wall Street Journal,* Mar. 12, 1996, cited by John Templeton, *Is Progress Speeding Up?* (Philadelphia, PA: Templeton Foundation Press, 1997), p. 80.

Page 182: [sidebar] "Effective teams huddle together..." Mr. Per, America's Confidence Coach™, www.everydayknowledge.com.

Page 183: "When people experience the wholeness..." from an interview with David Creelman, HR.com's ebulletin, July 9, 2001.

[sidebar] "Giants stand together..." Mr. Per, America's Confidence Coach™, www.everydayknowledge.com.

"Your job is to facilitate and illuminate..." John Heider, The Tao of Leadership (New York: Bantam, 1986), p. 113.

Page 184: "...individual emotional intelligence has a group analog..." Vanessa Urch Druskat and Steven Wolff, "Building the Emotional Intelligence of Groups," *Harvard Business Review,* vol. 79, no. 3, © 2001 by The Harvard Business School Publishing Corporation; all rights reserved.

"Another study of 62 management teams..." Daniel Goleman, Richard Boyatzis and Annie McKee, *Primal Leadership: Realizing the Power of Emotional Intelligence* (Boston: Harvard Business School Press, 2002), pp. 14-15.

Page 185: "Motivation and inspiration energize people..." John Kotter, "What Leaders Really Do," *Harvard Business Review,* vol. 79, no. 11, © 2001 by The Harvard Business School Publishing Corporation; all rights reserved.

Page 187: "There is an implicit, and I think wrong, assumption..." Charles O'Reilly III, from interview with David Creelman, HR.com's ebulletin, Jan. 29, 2001.

Page 190: [sidebar] "[Communication is] based on the same root as communion..." Frederick F. Reichheld, *Loyalty Rules! How Today's Leaders Build Lasting Relationships* (Boston: HBS Press, 2001), p. 154.

Page 191: "Leadership is autobiographical..." Noel M. Tichy, "Personal Histories: Leaders Remember The Moments And People That Shaped Them," *Harvard Business Review,* vol. 79, no. 11, © 2001 by The Harvard Business School Publishing Corporation; all rights reserved.

"Leaders have an enormous impact..." Daniel Goleman, Richard Boyatzis and Annie McKee, *Primal Leadership: Realizing the Power of Emotional Intelligence* (Boston: Harvard Business School Press, 2002), p. 222. Reprinted by permission of Harvard Business School Press. Copyright © 2002 by Daniel Goleman, all rights reserved.

"For thousands of years wise leaders have known..." Frederick F. Reichheld, *Loyalty Rules! How Today's Leaders Build Lasting Relationships* (Boston: HBS Press, 2001), p. 180.

Page 191: "We have found that the most effective persuaders..." Jay Conger, "The Necessary Art of Persuasion," *Harvard Business Review,* vol. 76, no. 3, © 2001 by The Harvard Business School Publishing Corporation; all rights reserved.

"The stories people tell about themselves..." Debra Meyerson, *Tempered Radicals: How People Use Difference to Inspire Change at Work* (Boston, MA: Harvard Business School Press, 2001), p. 113. Reprinted by permission.

Page 192: "If there ever was a time for businesspeople to learn..." Jay Conger, "The Necessary Art of Persuasion," *Harvard Business Review,* vol. 76, no. 3, © 1998 by The Harvard Business School Publishing Corporation; all rights reserved.

Page 193: "Any leader who thinks that a memo..." Steven B. Sample, *The Contrarian's Guide to Leadership* (San Francisco: Jossey-Bass, 2002), p. 149. Copyright © 2002 by Steven B. Sample. This material is used by permission of John Wiley & Sons Inc.

Page 194: [sidebar] "One of Warren Bennis' axioms..." Steven B. Sample, "The Art and Adventure of Collaborating with Warren Bennis," *USC Trojan Family Magazine,* Autumn 2000.

Chapter 9: Leadership is Action

Page 199: [sidebar] " It's about the equivalent of a Ritz..." from "Social Studies," *The Globe & Mail,* Dec. 3, 2002, p. A28.

"We go through cycles..." Interview by David Creelman, from HR.com's eBulletin, July 29, 2002.

INDEX

D

E

F

G

H

I

J

K

L

M

U

V

W

More Praise for *The Leader's Digest*

"*The Leader's Digest* is an easy and very inspiring read. Jim has managed to condense and concentrate the many perspectives, research, and wisdom on leadership into a highly digestible format that allows each reader to customize the book to his or her own needs and interests."
PETER URS BENDER, AUTHOR OF *LEADERSHIP FROM WITHIN*

"Remarkably thoughtful, provocative and useful. Jim has captured the collective wisdom on leadership from the world's greatest experts and thinkers, and encapsulated it in an exciting to read, comprehensive digest, using examples that will turn average Managers into great Leaders."
JOSEPH SHERREN, CANADA'S CORPORATE HEALTH GURU, CO-AUTHOR, *VITAMIN C FOR A HEALTHY WORKPLACE*

"In a clear voice that rings true, Jim Clemmer brings you an insightful, yet common sense, approach to everyday leadership dilemmas. This book will guide you into the learning that will turn leadership challenges into opportunities for growth. As you continue to refer to it, this book will be come a 'trusted advisor' that will continue to deepen the integrity of your leadership practice."
HUBERT SAINT-ONGE, KNOWLEDGE MANAGEMENT EXPERT AND CEO, KONVERGE DIGITAL SOLUTIONS

"*The Leader's Digest* is an excellent traveling book for today's busy executive. It is filled with common sense leadership advice built upon solid research. The book's easy to read format spiced with humor makes for pleasurable learning and provides the inspiration to turn its common sense principles into common leadership practice."
Bob Brennan, President, ServiceMaster Canada

"This book is a stirring compilation of wisdom regarding leadership. It assembles thoughts from incredibly diverse sources and makes them understandable and capable of being applied. No one can read it without learning (or re-learning) some important lessons about leadership."
JOHN H. ZENGER, VICE CHAIRMAN, NOVATIONS GROUP

"Jim Clemmer is a wise and special man. His insights into leadership are powerfully illustrated in his newest work The Leader's Digest. Learn from him . . . I do!"
DR. PETER LEGGE, CSP, CPAE, LL.D. (HON)